I0713892

The Fifty-Rand Note

and Other Short Stories

TSITSI NOMSA NGWENYA

2nd edition published in Great Britain in 2023 by:

Carnelian Heart Publishing Ltd
Suite A
82 James Carter Road
Mildenhall
Suffolk
IP28 7DE
UK

www.carnelianheartpublishing.co.uk

Paperback ISBN: 978-1-914287-06-0
E-book ISBN: 978-1-914287-39-8

1st published in Zimbabwe in 2017 by Royal Publishing House

A CIP catalogue record for this book is available from the British Library.

This collection of short stories is a work of fiction. The names, characters and incidents portrayed in it are the work of the author's imagination. Any resemblance to actual persons, living or dead, is purely coincidental.

Cover design & Layout:
Rebeca Covers

Typeset by Carnelian Heart Publishing Ltd
Layout and formatting by DanTs Media

Contents

My family both the living and the departed
Your love has been my shield,
your patience, courage
and strength, my sword.
I am deeply indebted to you
forever; *izandla zidlula ikhanda*.

For the entrepreneurs
whose lifetime savings were burnt to ashes,
who woke up without salaries for their workers,
scolded, even manhandled
by their angry employees;

For the workers who were there too
when everybody's hard earned cash
was controlled by cash barons

The Fifty-Rand Note

I come out of Sandy Springs Gardens on a warm Saturday morning, headed to Tshepisong Township in Soweto. The block of flats is at the corner of Vard Merwe and Klein Street, just across Number Four Police Station, Hillbrow, Johannesburg. My sister's husband offered to drive me to Tshepisong in his Bakkie but I declined. I am walking down Vard Merwe Avenue leisurely with my niece Ntombi and nephew Philani. A street advert catches my eye: "Get rich quick charms, Sangoma from Chipinge, Zimbabwe. Penis enlargement."

Wares are being sold by the roadside: belts, woollen hats, curios and watermelons. An old, heavy woman sits on a stool with her back covered in a blanket. She is wearing a red beret and does not move. Another woman with a face decorated the Xhosa way chats to a friend in a big frilled frock. The frills lift off her skirt, blocking her from direct contact with anyone. She re-arranges her vegetables on her stall and wipes her hands on the frills. The fourth woman in the row serves some fat cooks to a client who takes them with a cup of steaming coffee in a big yellow cup.

A man in dreadlocks shows a customer some wooden artefacts from a stall. He speaks in a hushed tone, frequently shaking his head, as if to get rid of irritating flies from his huge mane. The customer takes a closer look at the wood carvings of Africa's Big Five. He puts the white rhino aside and takes the elephant. A young man flashes across the street with several people in hot pursuit, firing obscenities in different languages. The stall keeper takes his gaze off the running boy and gives the customer the wooden king of the jungle. The customer refuses it for its unconvincing size. A friend from a nearby stall comes to the rescue with an offer of more royal dimensions. The customer pays and in addition, he is given a small tiger, India's pride, as a token of appreciation. The customer turns to look at a woman selling beads before disappearing into the crowd.

A pile of books by the street corner claims my attention. Steamy, detective and sci-fi genres but hardly any African literature. I lose interest. My mind drifts down Klein St.

A very beautiful woman in her early twenties comes into focus. She is wearing a few centimetres long skirt, raised further up by her curves. She chews some gum as she chats with a middle-aged man with a gold tooth and an earring on his left earlobe. The man is wearing his cap sideways. He lifts his fingers from his mouth and casually blows mushrooms of smoke into the sky. The man and woman disappear into a clothing shop.

I decide to buy the nieces and nephews I am visiting some delicacies from a supermarket within the mall. My eyes linger on some biscuits, candy, cake and fruits.

I notice a fat man behind the laundry shelf scratching the security codes off an item. His eyes are darting back and forth. He is wearing a big black jacket. I open a fridge and take out a Red Bull to recharge myself for the imminent ups and downs on Jo'burg streets. Ntombi carries the cake and Philani, the other stuff. I drain the energy drink and feel instantly refreshed.

We walk towards KFC. We enter to friendly greetings from the waitresses. Before we are served, three gay couples enter the restaurant. Two sets are white and sound British. The black couple moves forward and read a menu. A girl calls from behind the counter to her friend in the kitchen, "*Tendai huya uone ngochani*!"

"*Ehe, shuwa, tiri ngochani*. It is true, we are homosexual," answers the cross-dressed half of the black couple, twitching his mouth, his voice sarcastically adjusted to a feminine pitch.

It is easy to discern why the compatriots are in South Africa. Back home, the president says people of their orientation are worse than pigs and dogs that can tell male from female. The party receives their order, walk as free as black Zimbabweans in 1980, and disappears into their Land Rover and Porsche.

"Monsieur Boubacar finally brought his fiancée, madam Dieynaba."

"You lie, pere Diara!"

"She flew in last night, I helped her move out of the flat he had been sharing with his Congolese friends, to pave way for his mad' mizelle."

"Know what, N'dole, my friend, on Monday, I am organising a ticket for my wife."

"What will you do with the beautiful local one you are staying with?"

"I am married. She knows I am married. I will organise a new place for my wife elsewhere."

"Fair enough, my *broda*, but it is funny how we fought these toubabs back home. Does it not look like we are following them down here in South Africa?"

One may not be reproached for concluding that the conversing pair might be from the Islands of Goree, even Mali or Gambia. They are walking ahead of us. We cross the traffic lights together and then they disappear into a Nigerian haberdashery after exchanging some pleasantries with the owner who stands by the entrance, soliciting customers.

In a hair salon next to the haberdashery, women plait different styles while their customers sit still, fidget or browse mechanically through magazines, chatting in different languages, though Nyanja dominates the conversations.

We move towards Wonderous bus terminus, our next station. As we cross to the other side, I hear angry gunshots behind me. People scurry in all directions for cover. Some flatten themselves against the wall. I dare to look and see yellow police trucks and heavily armed police details everywhere. The shooting goes on for about ten seconds.

Oranges, apples, and other fruits remain a proper mess on the pavements after being trodden on by people running for dear life. Ntombi and Philani pull at me so we can disappear but, due to curiosity, I do not budge. I sense that danger is out of the way. Some people file into shops, and the looting begins. What a chance! The food house I have been to just few seconds ago is suddenly packed with street kids and adults, munching on chicken and chips. They do not care for the salads. Women run about, some clutching and pulling at young babies.

"It was a bank robbery."

"No, it was in a clothing shop."

"I was there when it started," says yet another expert.

"*Sisi shesha, kunzima la eGoli.*"

"They did not catch them, they were so swift..."

"They got two of the six robbers. The other four ran away with bags of cash in a black bag."

"The robbers got away. The police killed two pedestrians and a man who sells music by the street corner near the bank."

"*Hayi bo, bhuti, kanjalo nje*?"

"*Kema* Zimbabwe, from the style of stealing."

"Some of them have magnets on their fingertips."

"The other night they raided the eating house where I work at three in the morning. I was on the night shift. They entered and ordered everyone onto the floor. They demanded the keys to the safe and took everything, including all the cooked food. The police came at six in the morning. Everything happened in about five seconds but to us, it was like a hundred years."

In the madness of the moment, a young mother comes running with a baby strapped on her back. She is complaining that someone has just splashed some water on her from behind. Her skirt is dripping wet.

She offers me her back as she unstraps the baby. I ask her to come around the wall which shelters the vendors from the public at the bus terminus. From the way she speaks English, I pick up her origins at once. As I take the lifeless baby from her back, she realises the wetness is actually blood, not water. The whole place rings with anger and sorrow.

"*Mai-we! Mwana'ngu kani! Ndotangira papi? Mai-we-e!* My baby! Where do I start?" She cries with her querulous thin voice in Shona, a language spoken in Zimbabwe.

"*Ke'ng mme?*"

"*Ngoane*!"

"*Nini ekomeli mwana, namoni abimeli makila na litoyi*? What happened to the baby, I can see blood dripping out of its ear?" a woman asks in Lingala. From her looks, she must be from Congo Brazzaville or the bigger Congo.

"*Ah! Angalia, vana piga mutoto navanduki! Angalia sikio yake inotaka damu, mungu wangu*, oh my God! What happened to the child's ear, there is blood dripping from its ear!" two women enquire in Kiswahili, almost at the same time.

They are very dark and beautiful with cosmetic lines cut on their faces. One has huge holes on her earlobes and artificial gaps in her front teeth.

"*Ndi chiani chachita kumwana uyo*? What happened to the baby?" a Zambian woman who has a baby strapped to her back inquires in Nyanja.

"*Tsohle di phomotse modimo oa ka*!" exclaims the Sotho woman who had come first.

The bullet had gone through the child's skull. The bleeding had been from the left ear. Two sisters come along to help carry the lifeless baby to a metre taxi nearby. The mother mourns quietly as her sweat runs cold on her. I tug fretfully at my hair as we proceed with our trip. I think of our crisis back home. We are indeed in the middle of a slump, but this here is a place of seedy misery.

"Dube, Meadowlands. One to five," calls the bus attendant. I ask one man in Zulu where the Tshepisong rank is. He points in the direction without speaking. I get into the back seat with my little companions and make myself comfortable. In no time, the thirty-five-seater coughs, grunts and whines out of the terminus into Main Reef.

The people outside seem to be in a perpetual rush. A priest or pastor walks on bare feet. He is dressed in traditional Zulu regalia. His aide is carrying a reed mat behind him. Another man walks in the opposite direction, dressed in Egyptian amulets. My niece tells me the one on bare feet belongs to a certain church which mixes African tradition and Christianity. She has forgotten the name of the church.

Conversations go on in the bus in different local

languages. There are no conductors in these buses. I take out my fare, a fifty rand note, and hand it over to the Xhosa woman who is in front of me. I tell her I am paying for three passengers in the back seat. She nods and passes it over to a Sotho woman with a baby on her lap. I am struck by her beautiful and flawless skin. I notice her wonderful even teeth as she smiles at her baby girl.

As we turn into Main Reef, the bus driver announces that everyone be given their money back as the collection is thirty rand short. The fare is ten rand for everyone seated. I am incredulous. I have not been given my twenty-rand change, either. I muster the courage to tell the driver I had not received my twenty rand despite having paid. The Xhosa woman confirms having received my money and passed it on. There is commotion on the bus. I decide to keep quiet. I cannot understand how someone could have pocketed the fifty rand note. I become sympathetic and conciliatory with the woman whose accent points to Zimbabwe, probably Kalanga. Most likely, she is from Plumtree or somewhere down in Matabeleland South. She occupies the front seat, next to the driver. The seat comes with the burden of collecting the bus fare. Half the bus suspects she has pocketed the money without saying it openly. She is Zimbabwean, after all. My niece Ntombi gets furious and I urge her to hold herself together.

"*Laat ons line*, back to the terminus," the driver commands.

"I gave my money to this lady in front of me, she can confirm," explains the other boy who looks like the township type from the *tsotsi* talk and mannerism. A Cape Coloured, from the fairness of his skin.

"*Ora nna*, you did not give me any money!" the Sotho woman throws away her hands in desperation.

"*My maar hoor my, strues* God; I gave you my twenty rand and you even passed me back the change."

"*Mor ena oa ka*, I did not see *sheleti yahaho*," she refuses again.

"*Eya mme*, do not worry, all is alright. No one would hold you responsible," interjects a fat woman occupying two seats.

"*Asseblief*, what does it matter anyway? Everybody, get your money before you get down from the bus," the driver says calmly as he parks his bus in the terminus.

"*Matata ke'ng Moruti oa ka*, what is the problem, my priest?" probes the terminus attendant, surprised our bus is back so soon.

"Somebody is not being honest with their bus fare, nx, and how I hate to use *kragdadigheid* on such matters!"

"*Phumani nonke ebhasini yami siqale kasha*! Get out of my bus all of you!" the instructor screams with vehemence in his voice.

A heavily scarred man who has been quiet in all the confusion, runs to the nearby toilets. His wife, who is equally scarred, with two front teeth missing, gets busy packing and unpacking her luggage. She opens and throws her hands in protest against whatever thief that is wasting her time. She is wearing a pinafore and a green woollen hat written South Africa, World Cup 2010 in white. The driver instructs that everyone be searched.

"How much money did you have before you boarded the bus?" he asks the scarred man who had run off to the lavatory.

"Fifty rand."

The man searches his shirt pocket and takes out the fifty rand note. He then puts both his hands in his pants pockets and produces another fifty rand note. Without saying anything, he hands me the other note. There is laughter as we all climb back onto the bus. The man and his wife sit side by side behind the driver and the bus moves away. There is neither uneasiness nor guilt written on their faces.

* * *

On the streets, life continues as usual. We drive past a cemetery of metal as we approach the vast open spaces wedging the city and the black townships. The bus fumes and roars. On the left are heaps and mountains of mine quarry from the disused mines. Egoli, the Europe of Africa. We depart from the idle land and enter the South Western Township, Soweto.

In Tshepisong we are met by boys kicking their balls in the dusty red soils.

"Themba, Kgomotso, Tshepo, here!"

"*Hayi bo*! Themba, *ushaya kanjani, bona liya phuza amafu*. No, Themba. What kind of a shot is that? Now the ball is flying into the clouds!"

Their ball bounces and lands in a yard where two teenage girls stand chatting. The one who looks fifteen and heavily pregnant kicks the ball out to the boys who clap and whistle in appreciation and mockery. She is wearing a pair of very short pants which just cover her curves. Her blouse covers half the tummy. Strings which were cut from below the bodice in a decorative manner hang loosely, exposing her protruding navel. She starts jumping and hopping about with her left leg raised from the ground. She throws a stone and then follows it, leaping like a frog. They are playing a game on some lines drawn on the ground. Her grandmother calls her from inside the house and the teenager disappears, still holding her stone in her left hand.

We walk across the streets with women wearing pinafores and berets, chatting with each other across their fences. I estimate the number of friendships massacred from these gossips. A grown man winks at a young girl who is walking alone. His determined gaze tells a story. Her short skirt reveals fine legs.

We cross a footpath and feel a fountain of coolness. I evade gazes from the young township boys whose trousers hang low below their waists, cutting across their bums. We walk in an Indian file, Ntombi leading the way. Across the bush, a small stream appears and meanders beyond. We get back to the dirt road and my eyes are suddenly attracted to a well-manicured, beautiful garden. It stretches across the street into a vast open space. I wonder who could be doing this as I have not seen a single patch of a vegetable garden from the time we alighted from the bus. Ntando told me there were no water problems in Tshepisong like we experience in the Golden Triangle back in Harare.

As we get closer, I am surprised to meet my cousin tending to yellow roses, grown together with bell-shaped petals, all in bloom. There is also a fusion of bougainvillea, petunias, salvia, red and white roses. At the bottom of these are well organised, little white stones bordered by red smooth ones. He later claims that he had brought them from ten miles away in a wheelbarrow. Their aroma is euphoric. There are guava and peach trees in the yard too.

There is much happiness as I meet with my cousins, some of whom I last saw a decade and a half ago, back in the village. I have two cousins staying in the cabins in my brother's backyard. My brother's wife comes out of her bedroom to greet me. We laugh and chat. The children are excited to see me. I am also ecstatic. I am not sure if the youngest is happy to see me or if it is for the KFC and cake. She is too young to recall me.

Laughter floats over my cousin's flowers. I put the greasy feast on the table for all. I order tea and a small piece of cake. In a moment, the hi-fi is switched on and turned full blast.

Dumi and Njabulo start dancing. Njabulo lights his cigar and puffs away despite my reservations. The children dance as freely as the weeds in the nearby stream. Their friends join in the fun. Ntombi films the small party with her camera phone. Their dancing is mighty. Shy as she is, my sister in-law joins in. She cannot help it.

The air in the house becomes too warm and we move outside. Women sit on the lawn and the boys enjoy their jive as we all cheer. In no time, two big women join us.

"*Likayi mme*?"

"*Ke' tang sisi, wena*?"

I love the language, but I struggle to say my greetings. Motlalepula, my high school friend from Botswana, had taught me afew words and phrases so I try to join them for sentences. I must be sounding vulgar because my sister-in-law covers her mouth with her hand and the other women roll in laughter. I do not mind.

My brother arrives from work in his German made car. He joins the happy mood. After the greetings, he drives to the Spaza to get more drinks and some meat for barbequing. Somebody brings a braai stand and in no time, the charcoal is glowing. It seems to me these folks have nothing more to their lives than stereos, beer bottles and braai stands. Everything seems to have been ready.

The older crew let beer flow through their veins like blood while music beats against the soles of their feet. The lifestyle they display ignites hope instead of gloom. They dance rhythmically in the language of animals that have no words but memory.

A heavily pregnant woman walks through the gate in the company of her husband. He joins the men whilst she joins the women in the shade of a peach tree. There are no introductions. We only greet each other.

"So, woman, you are so big now! Who is the father of this one you are carrying?"

"Do you need to ask ma? It's still in the kraal isn't it?" she replies with a naughty wink.

They all break into a knowing mischievous laugh. All the while, my sister- in-law looks down in shame, trying in vain to stop the juicy tales.

"My Mozambican live-in lover beat me to a pulp last night after he caught me with the taxi driver," laughs a woman who had come in after the pregnant sister.

"You cannot be such a fool to be assaulted by a Mozambican in this country."

"Get township dogs on him and get him deported," advises the pregnant sister.

"I wouldn't dare. Who would pay my rent and give me money to send my children to school?"

"*Uyateta khona eZim ne*?" laughs the newcomer.

"Shush, Themba will hear this and slaughter me. I am told there is no water and painkillers in their hospitals."

"But *uyatsiba*, he knows the pregnancy is his, isn't it?"

"You must have been cooked in a fool's pot, *setlatla sa*

mosadi!" shouts a woman with a gold tooth and freckles.

"Oh, yes he does, but he wouldn't dare come to my husband. I told him to stay away. I see him in a hotel every time he comes for his business dealings and it is normally during the day."

"Sekuru's daughter-in-law," laughs the talkative newcomer. The other woman who had been quiet all the time lifts her skirt to show us the knife scars from her husband who found her in bed with a Nigerian lover. Since then, she claims, she has stopped her philandering ways. She says the husband adores her still.

I take a stroll to the garden outside the yard, across the street. Lively carrots, beetroot, potatoes and spinach greet me. There are raspberries and gooseberries too. I look across and see idle township boys walking up and down the narrow meandering foot paths that criss-cross and disappear into the low-lying stream on my right. Some boys emerge from the stream, puffing coils of smoke through their nostrils, laughing uncontrollably, their eyes blood-red. Some of them walk like reversing cars, oblivious of everything.

On the side of the street where there are no brick houses, there are tin shacks. Their walls appear dwindled from the load they are carrying. There are used mattresses, razor wire and bicycles, ready to be taken to Tsholotsho and Kezi by Nhlanhla the local *malayitsha*. He also transports mealie-meal, sugar and onions to relatives in Bulawayo.

People come to buy vegetables from us as we stand

chatting. They are harvested as and when a client requires them. My brother who grows them was an Agriculture teacher back home. He is not yet employed because he has no work permit. I enjoy the air for its odour and surprise. Here, water is not sporadic or apologetic like back home, despite dams filling up every rainy season.

A young, curvy lady joins us. Her lips are glossed with lemon scented balm. She is chewing bubble-gum with a hint of cinnamon. I am struck by her impatience. She folds her hands, seeking consolation, not warmth, maybe something to restrain her impatience because today, unlike other winter afternoons, it is fairly warm. Her gold tooth flashes as she whispers something to my brother. There are no introductions, but after a brief exchange of words with him, she relaxes and greets me again. I smile at her as I show her silent acknowledgement. It is a silent language we both understand as women.

Back in the yard, there are more women, sitting and chatting. Excited voices and loud music spill onto the lawn under my feet. I give my niece and nephews some coins as I prepare to leave. The little girl holds the money I gave her in a tight fix, most probably thinking of buying some potato crisps. There is much sadness as I announce my departure. I feel like crying as the children swarm and cling to me like bees. I assure them of my love and tell them that I shall return.

"*Askies, sisi*, so, how long have you been in South Africa?"

asks a neighbour who is having her hair plaited by Ntombi.

"Oh, I came on Friday morning and I am returning tomorrow."

"I feel sorry for you. The journey is too long. The last time I travelled to Musina I had my feet swollen for the whole week. I thought you had come to look for a job or you were working somewhere here already. Which bus are you taking?"

"She flew in and is flying back, you whore!"

"*Matata ke'ng tu*, I am asking, fela."

"So, when are you visiting again?" asks the pregnant sister.

"Anytime I get a chance. I come to South Africa almost twice every month for business. Sometimes I proceed to Cape Town and Port Elizabeth."

"Auntie, may you please bring some books. You always carry some in your bag?" little Dumi asks as he opens my handbag to take Achebe's *Arrow of God*.

"And me too, and me too, me too," goes the chorus from all my nieces and nephews who are still clinging to me.

"Oh yes, I will bring something for your age, dear friends. You will get this one from my library when you are older."

"*Kiyareboha*, aunty, *utsamaye sinhle*."

We arrive at a place of incense and style, driven in the old Germany-manufactured vehicle as the sun dips into its mother's belly. On elevated ground, under the raised balconies, stand very beautiful women, advertising their God-given wares. The demand seems to be there for the world's oldest profession. Most of the ladies are almost in the nude. Children need to be fed and sent to school. Even some husbands need to be fed too. I feel ashamed as I am walking with my brothers, niece and nephew. I decide I will come back for a stroll with my brother-in-law later after my brothers depart for Tshepisong.

Two policemen drag two gentlemen into a yellow van near a night club. A woman pulls my brother-in-law aside and tells him how handsome he looks. She holds his arm for a while, eyeing him directly in his face with the eyes of an eagle. I stand aside, motionless and voiceless. He pulls away from her after thanking her for the compliment. She tightens her brassiere as she vomits obscenities from a mouth whose lipstick could hold a glass of beer unaided. The air is filled with disaster. I ask my brother-in-law that we walk back home to Sandy Springs.

A bald-headed man fries some chicken livers in an open pan by the street corner from a gas stove. Next to him, one sister cooks pap and another slices vegetables and packs them away, probably for resale. A young widow sells some chicken feet to a middle-aged man wearing a security uniform. She has baby twins who appear to be at the crawling stage, one in her lap while the other makes paddling motions with her little arms, trying to climb on her lap too. Her black headscarf moves backward to show her beautiful hair underneath. She must be in her mid-twenties. More women sit along the street with huge steaming pots.

"*Lekani ndigule mbale ya nsima ndi nsomba kuti ndibele*

njala. Let me buy a plate of pap and fish to cheat this hunger," a man says to his friend as they walk side by side.

"*Gula nsima ndinkhuku. Samaphika nsomba monga mmene muna zolowera ka ku Malawi moti ukhonza sanza utatha kudya chakudya cho*. Just buy pap and chicken because these people do not prepare fish the way you are used to back in Malawi. You may even throw up after eating it," the other man advises as they move towards the women with huge pots.

We meet my brother-in-law's friend from work and I politely greet him in English. He answers in a Venda-laced accent. We chat for a few moments before he dashes away.

Two gentlemen enter the bar like fugitives. A gun blasts down the street but people continue with their normal business. I am startled and scared. Death so near, so close to the skin you could smell it. I feel I am at the mercy of misfortune. The ladies from the oldest profession line the streets, seemingly unafraid. They are aged between fourteen and twenty-five. Most are strikingly beautiful. I wonder about their origins. Where are their mothers, brothers and sisters?

"It is your money which determines the time you want with me," one of the ladies wearing a belt for a skirt, shouts to a client.

The client is a well-groomed gentleman sporting a shiny gold ring on his second finger. After a few whispers, they disappear around the corner into an Isuzu double-cab with yellow number plates. Her sweet perfume floats in the air.

Johannesburg lights converse with clusters of stars. A woman enters a car and quickly disappears into the cruel night. Night of intoxicating brightness. A heavy thud follows a scream. And then silence. Some people cheer from a fifteenth-floor balcony. A woman screams. A baby cries. A man has just landed on top of plastic plates of fruits, already dead.

A few passers-by take a look and carry on with their normal business. I shudder and shiver. My brother-in-law tells me to walk quickly and disappear from the scene. I hesitate. Maybe the fallen man needs help. Maybe he is not dead. But I am afraid to look back in case I morph into a pillar of salt. I walk in lethargic silence. I try to close off my fears by thinking of my days as a young girl, playing with my sisters by the river back in the village. It shuts out the horrors, but only for a moment. I go back again and see our little bodies squirming in the cold water we swam in in the afternoons, sure to stay adequately hidden from herd boys and hornbills swooping above our tiny heads, above rocks and above Mphafa trees lining the riverbanks. We swim in all the colours of sunlight. We bask in the sun like lazy lizards, slowly, satisfied.

We pass another spot and the ladies are still busy. "Fifty rand for a short time, I can give you a discount since you are from up north," negotiates one fallen goddess to a young man. It was as if his origins were inscribed in his palms as she held them.

An old bald man comes out of a BMW. He sports gold chains on his neck and wrists, and gold rings on all his fingers. He pulls the girl to the car without a word. The jilted suitor lands on him like a leopard and in no time, there is blood everywhere. His entrails peep from his open belly. His friends pull him to his car and drives away. I am startled at the ease of tragedy. I close my eyes to slow the flood of terror.

The darkness is fluid. I have persuaded my brother-in-law to take me back before I see worse things. Now I am counting the stars from my sister's balcony.

The brilliance of the Johannesburg lights outshines the moon and the stars. The sight of the lights across the sky from the seventeenth-floor apartment is enigmatic. They separate the land from the skyscrapers, the sky and the people; people who are always in a perpetual rush, who appear as if they are ready to depart all the time, day and night. Bright colours, bright lights, gold teeth, knives, guns. Johannesburg. But the sky is as still as heated air from the abandoned noise at the bottom. Excited voices and loud music spill onto the pavement under my feet. Nigerians, Congolese, Zambians rule the streets. Some Zimbabwean intellectuals lead the industry – former female Zimbabwean civil servants mopping floors and minding babies. Some of their male counterparts pick grapes and tend to gardens in the suburbs, *emakhishini*. Women sell wares and their crafts to bring groceries to homes which are double-storey houses furnished with fear and hunger, thirst and dark nights.

I am told that every Friday night, minibuses depart to the Sovereign State, pulling trolleys from eSibayeni. ESibayeni is a fenced enclave within the skyscrapers where *malayitshas* park their minibuses waiting for passengers and groceries to be sent home. The place is usually full of *tshangani* bags with groceries packed on top of the skeletons of men and women who die from a disease with no name. It is never mentioned, much less at funerals. It used to scream its presence a few years back but these days it can be difficult to tell the sick from the healthy. The anti-viral medication is now available to all the people. If the disease is dreaded elsewhere, here it is not. Fifty rand is for those using protection and hundred rand is for each live encounter.

I scarcely close my eyes at night.

I spend the Sunday indoors because my flight is cancelled by Air Zimbabwe with no explanation. I decide to go back to my sister's place than stay at a hotel indefinitely. I need company and family. I live in isolation in Harare, most relatives far away from me. I feel lonely every time I am weighed down by business. I need a break. Our savings have disappeared in banks, eroded by inflation, high blood pressure rising with it. Some people die alongside the Zimbabwean dollar. Those who survive live for their debts.

My cousin who visits me that Sunday teaches at a high school here. She says she has two killers in her class. One boy murdered his step-father for beating the boy's mother to a pulp and another murdered his classmate with a knife at break time. She says there are four pregnant girls in her class. Her story reminds me of my former classmate who fell pregnant and committed suicide out of shame when we were in form three. She had broken the school record which stood at twenty-five years without such a thing happening.

My flight is rescheduled for Monday at seven in the morning. At least I can be in the office by half past eight. Better, I think. My cousin who lives in Soweto volunteers to take me to the airport together with my nephew. My cousin's husband works in Pretoria. He wakes up at three in the morning to take three trains before he arrives at the restaurant where he works as a cleaner in the morning and a waiter later in the day, earning one thousand five hundred rands. He is a qualified accountant with CIS. At home he lived comfortably with his family in a four-bedroom house in Matsheumhlope, Bulawayo. Their daughter is currently at the University of Zimbabwe, studying for a degree in Animal Science. Her brother is at a boarding school. My sister is not working. The factory that had employed her for fifteen years shut down just before the introduction of the multicurrency system. They are renting out their house in Bulawayo now for their children's school fees. My sister lives on subsistence farming in the village and selling stuff she comes to order here in South Africa from time to time.

We get to O.R. Airport at half past five. I check in but my flight is not showing on the electronic notice board. I send in my bag and start to shop around after persuading my companions not to leave me alone in case our only aircraft has a fault or something happens to it. Pilots could be on strike again. Endless possibilities.

It is eleven in the morning now. Word is the plane is delayed. Phones buzz from my office. I am hounded by creditors. The bank has no money. Service providers have gone to lawyers and debt collectors. Most employees have not reported to work.

Employers are living on their nerves. How do you manage people you have not paid? Some sell this and that during working hours and still want to be paid by the end of the month. I follow up on clients and investors. They tell me that they are still deciding, weighing down the obvious risks. I am almost giving up on them. What has pushed me from day to day is hope. Hoping for the best and preparing for the worst. Anything that comes in between can no longer surprise me.

It is three in the afternoon and my flight is still delayed. There are more women in the restroom waiting for the same flight. The women leave their babies home on the bottle to trade across the continent. It is them who hold together the last threads of the Zimbabwean economy. This group at the airport had been brought by the South African Airways from China. They had been waiting for our Zimbabwe aircraft which was delayed by forty-eight hours without explanation. They had not seen bath water in three days before they decided to dry wash in the toilets.

"*MaZimbabweans kea a tena, a tletse gohle mo, babangwe ba sadi ba gona ke ba le bahlapela ka mola dintlwaneng tsa basadi. Ke gore re ba romele go papago bona*. These Zimbabweans are a nuisance, all over the show. Some of the women were bathing in the lady's toilet. Just let them go."

I smile the smile of those who do not cry as a cleaner complains to a man who appears to be her senior. She comes close to me to emphasise the foolishness of the women in the toilet, now speaking in Zulu. I reply her with a smile again as I dry my hands.

After an hour, we are led to Gate 77. A free South African aircraft will be organised to take us to Harare. We all walk to the departure lounge, quietly.

"I wonder when Africans will learn that we did not have boundaries in Africa some hundred years ago," says a man to nobody in particular. People look at him and do not answer.

I meet my old friend, Zinzile, with her pilot husband who is now flying South African Airways. We greet each other and hold our peace. She tells me they are visiting their home in Harare. I look out to watch planes landing and taking off, a soothing pastime now. Most people in the departure lounge display an unquenchable sorrow and sedentary postures, with only fragments of dignity left. The unscrupulously ambitious and unswervingly egocentric individuals have drained the nation's blood. My thoughts somersault deeper into misery. I even imagine the ruins of Parthenon and the thought leaves me in the deep end of my strength.

We walk into the waiting shuttle bus like spring water flowing to the desert, ready to disappear into vast sands, with no smiles or curses. Our dignity is neither here nor home, but in a past that is now hard to remember. We are going to cup our sovereignty with our hands and sip it like water in an hour's time.

We climb the big bird's ladder with raw wounds and butchered minds. The big bird runs down the runway, facing the Atlantic Ocean and then turns before gathering speed. It heaves its heavy body up north, cutting through fluffs of clouds, leaving Johannesburg's hectic life down under.

I pull my single small suitcase out of the airport, to meet my daughter and niece.

I give my niece the fifty rand note for fuel as her car is on Empty.

Yesterday Morning

I did not sleep well on Friday night. Dogs were barking at invisible beings outside my window. I heard footsteps and felt a presence at my bedroom window. I had been drifting in and out of sleep to try and see these beings to no avail. I could only see stars darting like night insects above and under the trees. I decided not to utter a word against the beings that the dogs were barking at.

Now I try hard to sleep. My heart is shredded by pain endured over the years that pulsates in my body. It beats so fast I wonder how it has survived in the blast furnace of my small body. The big men dug pit latrines and they left them uncovered. We are now falling into them. I am properly stressed. I wish I had not got into business in the first place. I am between a rock and a hard economy. Every day I fight wars. Scars run too deep to be erased. I have resigned to deep solitude, to look at the deep scars of my soul more closely. They all phone, text and email me. I do not know what to tell them anymore. My strength is flagging. My body is giving in.

I have lost everything. I have sold everything to pay debts which could still not be cleared. Last week I lost the car. Yesterday it was the office furniture. Our landlord is threatening to kick us out. I borrowed money to keep the company doors open so that nobody would lose their jobs. So that we all could send our kids to school, house and feed them. Someone told me to cry away the nightmares. She told me to cry my pain away. Not all crying leads to mourning; not all bleeding leads to death, she assured me. I have bled and cried. If I am not dead, then I am only alive for the pain.

I worry about the future of my children. I could die from this pain. My soul is giving in, sinking under the weight of my heavy heart. What could be still functioning normally? Do not think too much, my voice calls at me from the ashes, a charred and tormented voice. Fear, my trusted companion, tells me I am doomed.

The walls of my room continue in immortal strength. My strength is nothing like walls. Walls are bricks and mortar, not flesh, bones and water. I can only carry so much.

It dawns. The dogs stop barking. I lie quietly. Employees demand money even if there was no business. They are employees. They have taken me to court before, but we were together as we watched our hard-earned money burn in the banks. We were together. Now they are fighting me.

"Sell your children and pay us," they scream.

"Go to the lavatory and money will come out so you may give us," they seem to say.

Their contracts indicate that they should be paid in Zimbabwean dollars. They have all forgotten that.

"You have been so strong all along, try to see the light. We shall make it. Stay positive like you have always been. I know you will make it," a friend encourages me from the other side of the receiver.

With her words, I try to realign my scrambled emotions. The matter of my children remains my anguish. Maybe I should go to England. Surely it is the itching foot that gives, not blankets and buttocks. To do whatever everyone is doing – bum cleaning. Where is the British High Commissioner's office? No, by the way we are out of the Commonwealth! We have our sovereignty, our land. But food and water remain our anguish. It rained last season. Dams are full. Remember to look for the British Embassy not the High Commissioner. I should decide before my remains congeal in the drawers of a mortuary.

The whole matter rankles in my mind. I look at the files piled in my bedroom, or where I sleep. I do not know what to call it, bedroom, study or office? But that is where I live and sleep. Even dream, read and hope.

I thank the Almighty for the shelter He is providing. Many souls are out there in the cold with the remains of their companies, wounded hearts and trashed dignity.

Blood sings from my thumping heart. I smell my own sweat. "It has been five years now. My nerves are breaking. Thank you, I will try," I assure my friend. I am crunched into a stain. The diamond character I possessed is almost gone.

There are moments I feel some numbness spreading from my left arm across my body and something goes quiet inside my head. My body feels like a discarded object. My nerves have vanished. My soul is burnt like dry leaves, so is my heart. My heart, a battlefield for the continent. My soul weaves through fires and thorns. I smell death, my own death like a fragrance. Pitch darkness as that of the night carries me away.

"Here, drink this, auntie," cries my niece.

"No, she will choke. Fan her," suggests my nephew.

"Let's pray," says my niece.

My emotions go taut like the strings of a guitar. I see myself walking with a lot of people I do not know. My soul floats to a field, my mother's field back in the village. My body is left behind. I see my dead sister on an anthill. I run to her. My dead brother emerges from behind the plain field among the maize stalks which were devoured by cattle and donkeys. He beckons me away, hiding his face from me. He too, died three years ago.

"Do not come to us! The children are alone. Do not come here. Go back. Go back and look after your children. They are all your children. Go back!" My sister hides her face. I identify her with her clothes and voice, body and posture standing on the anthill. I see my knees trembling from my charred soul, my half dead body. I float between the clouds. My soul comes back to my body through a small aperture. My breath rises like a swimmer's. I hold it until my senses are alight. My soul glides, incandescent like a waterfall. There is the force of air pounding down my lungs causing me to fall dizzily. I try to mutter a word. I fall into a deep sleep-in dream.

I am back in the village where I grew up, at my uncle's

homestead which was destroyed two decades ago. Today his huts stand in their places, all of them firm like beehives. He died a decade ago. I am in a dagga-and-thatch hut and I am sick. I am confused. I am guarded by an aunt who earned a reputation as a witch in my family because of her strange behaviour which was always laced with cruelty. She is with her daughter in their kitchen which I remember from a long time ago. It has been moved to the side of my dead uncle's homestead. There are women all over the yard. I recognise most of them. They are waiting for my death. I am very cold. They do not want to enter the kitchen I am put in. I am lying on a reed mat without blankets to cover my weary body. Someone has lit a fire to warm me. They are waiting to mourn and slaughter a goat, maybe a cow, whatever. I say inaudible statements, all mixed up in a dream. My mind is perforated like a dry leaf. My limbs are stiff. I feel like an exhumed body.

A fiery odour like abandoned memories catches my breath. I jump out of the hut. Out, out, out away from the mourners. Outside, under a tree, I see a man I cannot identify wearing a black jacket. He waves at me.

"This one has failed me. I have failed. I surrender. She prays, I can't have her," he screams at a woman without looking at me. There is silence among the waiting mourners.

My phone rings. I answer it.

"Get away from those people! They are the same that want you dead. Quick, quick, get away from there now!" warns the caller.

Without answering, I float, leaving everybody behind. I see them from the sky, still waiting for my return. I fly with my body. The commitment in my bones encourages me, making me feel like a fossil floating in noonday light. I land on the second floor of a beautiful house. I hear the voices of the waiting women. My phone rings again.

"Get out of that place. They are the same people waiting to devour you. Get out at once!" screams the caller again.

I feel revulsion so deep my body jumps forward. I feel the explosion in my head. I am started like an engine. Thoughts gather in my memory like a whirlwind.

I see my body in a room.

My niece is singing a hymn. My nephew is praying. My body is still and no longer vibrating. My limbs are stiff. My soul comes back to my body, slowly, ethereally. The umbilical presence between my body and soul is at first my children and then debts. My soul will have peace once those are sorted. My soul moves, passing through the field. I see my maternal grandmother standing on a slight rise, besides a tree. She opens her hands and arms for me and I run to her. Her face changes to that of my mother but with wrinkled hands, the flesh on the arm flabby but showing a fresh face, a younger looking face.

There is not a green blade of grass left in the fields from the scathing sun. Everything has been burnt to cinders. It is a lean year. The barbed wire tangles in my mind. My dreams still cling defiantly to my heart and mind. There are drought fissures to where my soul is clinging to my mother or grandmother. Relentless, fierce winds blow into my being. Suddenly there is rain. Cats and dogs. In the next few seconds, the whole field turns green. Maize, sorghum and millet compete for the sun as they show flowers of corn heads, ready to produce. Legumes also compete for space under their stalks. The pumpkin plants display yellow flowers, and the cow beans, their dazzling white and purple flowers. My grandmother or mother smiles at me as she shows me my new field, a successful field, as she departs into it.

I open my eyes and I see my niece and nephew sitting by my side on my bed. They are startled and relieved.

"Have some food, auntie," pleads my nephew.

"No, I will bath first."

I eat rice and soup after bathing. Slowly, my strength comes back. If only they knew, they would forgive us. I am a tormented soul with hope still hanging like dew on pumpkin leaves.

A Dollar for Two

As the red sun comes out from behind the canopy of trees, piercing my eyes like a needle, I walk to the bus stop with a tired step. The sky is clear. I walk an uphill path to reach a shimmering flatness in the heart of Harare's Golden Triangle. Air pounds down my lungs. I try not to smell the fiery odour of the memories I want to forget. I try to bury my hurt in a steady zeal. I walk with my heart and limbs, not with my soul. My soul is floating somewhere, the way spiders walk on water. I am going to search for the peace which has eluded me like a man I met in a vision. The little eggs of hope that remain in people are being crushed under the boulders in the Golden Triangle where the rich and affluent reside, or where they used to reside before fleeing to live in squatter camps in South Africa. Some of the people went as far as Netherlands. They are scattered all over the world, as far as Syria and Macedonia. Not that they wanted it.

A water delivery truck drives past and their assistants holler at me, mocking me for not having a car while being dressed like I belong here, in the Golden Triangle. I forgive them. I don't want their voices to burn my already burnt nerves. I move towards the bus stop which is the shade of a tree.

I stand under the Musasa. Here, water is sold for fifty dollars per five thousand litres. In the Golden Triangle. It is a thriving business but those who sell the water deny that they sell the God-given liquid. They say the money is a charge for fuel and their time. They would never sell water. The five thousand litres do not last one and a half weeks for an average family of six. Water.

Those with no tanks and no money to buy water are seen from time to time pushing wheelbarrows filled with all types of containers including pots, anything that can hold water. Some maids balance twenty litre plastic containers like Stone-Age village women. The only difference is that they wear tight jeans and hipsters, their hair long and shiny, like that of white women. They descend with their purple and yellow hair from double and triple-storey houses, carrying tins as they speak in borrowed American and English accents. The water they are fetching has new uses now, unlike during the Stone Age. In the Golden Triangle.

In most yards there are no green lawns to speak of anymore. Some tall and heavily grass peeps and hangs out from brick boundary walls. In yet some yards you find only the brown blades of grass, dead leaves under gigantic trees and dead golden maize stalks from the previous farming season. We now do a lot of farming in and outside our yards, in any free space. We also dump our rubbish, in rocky terrains and swampy vleis. We grow maize in the warm soil here and let the soils of the farms we repossessed miles from here tighten back to their virginity. We are here in The Golden Triangle.

Suddenly, there are two women by the bus stop, one of them given to too much talking. She keeps on silencing her colleague with a lot of gesticulated emphasis. The talkative one is plump and pouting. There is a bucket with something constantly attracting flies, big green ones. She waves her fat hand over the bucket until she finally places her handbag on top of it. I am not sure if that will keep the flies away. She is wearing a bright coloured top, not very old, not quite new either, her rings of dried and fresh sweat visible under her armpits. Her voluminous skirt flies and rests on top of the handbag. She has beautiful, short natural hair.

The other woman, tall and slender, is wearing a Zambian outfit even though she appears local. Her beautiful features seem to have been hardened by maternity. She habitually smooths her skirt with her hands as she listens to her friend. She nods her head to what her friend is saying. She must be fertile ground for her friend's damaging words.

The talkative friend does not seem to have a good word on her tongue. She looks restless even when she is quiet. Her mop of a wig falls in strands as she does so, covering her right eye. She keeps rearranging it with her palm. I do not go near them, unwilling to catch their superstition and destruction.

A miserable hearse of a taxi stops near the two babblers. It looks like the driver has dropped a client nearby and of course, he cannot leave the precious greenback along the way. He offers us a ride with the same commuter omnibus fare we were waiting for. I walk to the taxi.

"The taxi is full now. As it is, we are already squashed," screams the fat woman.

"She can still find space, the back seat takes three people," pleads the taxi driver.

"We are squashed, *mukwasha*. She can wait for a commuter omnibus. I have this bucket of fish as well so we can't fit in."

"In a commuter omnibus you are made to squeeze each other four by four on three-seater seats."

"As you said, this is not a commuter, she is not riding in here," mumbles the slender woman.

"Sorry, *maiguru*. You could have made yourself comfortable but your friends are refusing."

"It's alright. l will catch the next lift." I lift my hands in surrender. An omnibus stops just behind the taxi.

"Thank you *maiguru* for showing presence of mind."

"So, we do not have minds? He, *mukwasha*?" fumes the plump woman, placing her bucket on the floor of the car.

"Copacabana, *maiguru* town, town. Hey you, taxi, we will get your licence revoked if you continue stealing our customers," shouts the conductor, his veins standing out of his face. The culprits quietly drive away. I enter the bus to join two others passengers. Along the way, we see an old man walking briskly along the road. He turns his head to look at our approaching bus. I quickly face the opposite direction as if l do not want anyone to know l am around.

"*Mdara*, get in. Let's go to town. We are going up to

Fourth
Street."

"I do not board buses that belong to poachers."

"We are not poachers *mdara*, let's go," the conductor pleads as he opens the door for him. The old man thinks for a while and then leaps in.

"Is the road ahead safe?" the driver shouts at his colleague who is driving in the opposite direction.

"No, they are at the corner of Harare Drive and Drew Road. Go the other way. They are also at that spot before the Glenara and Enterprise robots."

"Town, town sister, Copacabana!" the conductor calls at two women walking by the side of the road. One is wearing a domestic servant uniform with a baby strapped to her back. The women look at the conductor and indicate that they are not going far.

"They belong to ZIFA, don't worry about them," explains the old man.

"Zimbabwe Footing Association."

"Uhm, yes, they are continuing with the association."

"Established 2005."

The commuter omnibus stops for a beautiful girl who appears to be a student at a nearby tertiary college. She clutches her books and does not immediately get in.

"Hey sister! Are you possessed? Why look at the bus as if you have a demon which needs to be appeased before it smells the diesel," the conductor shouts with his harsh, foul, almost asphyxiating breath spreading all over. One can be forgiven for thinking that a skunk stays in his mouth and another under his armpits.

"I only have three rands and I really need to go," pleads the girl.

"Let's go, but don't do it again tomorrow."

"Are you going to give her the bus fare for tomorrow then?" questions the old man.

"I am not her father, old man, and this is my office. I am at work!"

"I sell these at work because I have not received my salary for the past six months." The old man lifts two pairs of plastic sandals from China.

"How much, *mdara*?" enquires the conductor?

"You get two pairs for a dollar."

"Let's see," a woman from the back seat extends her hand to the conductor, who passes them on to her. "They are nice but *mari handina*."

"I could have afforded four pairs in a day if I had kept my job of picking grapes in the Western Cape, ha ha!" laughs the driver.

"Oh, so you are also a Diaspora. I came back in early 2010. I was in KwaZulu-Natal."

"*Mdara*! You too crossed the borders!" exclaims the conductor.

"What was I going to feed my family with? I was also earning what everybody was earning. I took a teaching job at a private college."

"Why did you then leave South Africa?"

"Besides earning peanuts, xenophobia. I won't even talk of the living conditions."

"Put your fares together. One dollar per two people, parents, I have no change," the conductor commands.

Four people get on the bus before the Chisipite roundabout. Two pay a dollar after sorting themselves out. A man pays four rands and five pula. Two more hop in before Nazareth House. One pays with a ten rand note, another with a five American-dollar note.

The bus moves on and stops for a young man who is flagging frantically.

"*Ndeipi*?" asks the young man as he enters the bus.

"*Tiribho*. Where are you coming from within this rich and affluent neighbourhood?"

"*Zvakapera izvo*. That is a myth now. These are suburbs for everyone," interjects a woman sitting next to the old man.

"Village people have better living conditions than most of these people now," echoes someone in the front seat.

"*Kumusha kwakauya kutown*. I got a room to rent in the main house somewhere near the shops," answers the young man finally.

"Ha, ha, ha!"

"He, he, he!"

"And your business of supplying water to that Complex?" asks the driver.

"It has become the business now. We charge a dollar for two by ten litres required on the first floor, doubling the price as we go up the floors."

"Where do you get the water from?"

"From the communal borehole within the Complex."

"The situation reminds me of Mozambique during Samora Machel's time, and how you used to laugh at them calling them all sorts of names!" the old man comments.

"Ha, ha, ha!"

"He, he, he!"

"Ho, ho, ho!"

A woman wants to alight at the corner of Arcturus and Enterprise Road. The conductor has no change yet, so he gives her a token for it. She can use it for her ride back. Tokens are laminated papers printed "fifty cents" on either side. There is no rising sun or Dr Martin Luther King Jr's head on them so we don't know if they are in Zimbabwean or American cents. The most important thing is that they serve their purpose.

"I need my money now. I need a coin. I can't take that token because I don't live here," complains the recipient.

"None of our business. Town, sister! Copacabana! If you do not want a token, then buy your own car. Town sister!"

"Copacabana, sure. I am going somewhere near Rainbow Towers."

"*Ka wani*, my sister."

"Hey, you! Stop lying to customers! There is no commuter

from this route which is allowed to rank at Copacabana!" shouts a conductor from another bus which has parked, waiting for passengers.

"Plough your own field, you scumbag!"

Upon hearing that, the young lady who does not want the token money leaves the drama scene to hitch hike for private cars.

"Let her go to private cars where women are sometimes forced to breastfeed frogs and snakes!"

"*Ndiwo ato maCompany acho*, he he he!"

"Ha, ha, ha the things people do in desperate times!"

"If you are not giving me my change, I would rather come with you to town then you can give me my change when we get there."

"Suit yourself and get inside quickly, woman. We don't have twenty hours to attend to your story." But before the woman sits down, the driver moves the bus so violently she hits the steely extension which is supposed to be a seat with a thud, the contents of her handbag spilling all over the bus.

"But you want our money!"

"My children will ask how my day was, just like yours. You too want the money," shouts the conductor after spitting through the window.

"You should at least have the decency to apologise. Do not insult her."

"I am not as educated as you are, but I take your children to school every day. You should also show me some respect."

There is a roadblock before the traffic lights. Two lady officers are signalling the driver to stop. The driver swerves from the road and stops the vehicle.

"Your papers!"

"You saw my papers, madam, on my way to Greystone Park. There is no point in showing them to you as nothing has changed yet. You gave us a ticket. Here it is, in case you have forgotten."

"I don't care! Go behind that truck over there," the police officer insists, pointing her finger at the truck.

"We saw those guys on their way to Greystone Park. We will deal with them if they ignore our instructions and come back from town without the required papers," reasons the male traffic officer.

"I have made my decision, I am sorry. Go behind the truck", the lady motions her hand as if shooing chickens from her grandmother's kitchen hut in the village.

The driver shoves his hands in his back pocket and follows behind the officer. He blows his noses into the folded fingers of his hands. A while later, he comes back into the vehicle with furrows of anger on his forehead.

"Eve's Squad."

"*Iqembu lika Eva.*"

"*Chikwata chaEva,*" echoes some male passengers in the bus. All the women look down with shame.

The driver mutters inaudible and unnameable obscenities as he starts to play a Thomas Mapfumo track on his radio.

"*Nyika yamaichemera yaita mamvemve.*"

The minibus is still not full. After the Newlands roundabout, two elderly women come on board. After the traffic lights, more people get on to the omnibus, filling it up. The driver stops and the conductor keeps on calling for more passengers.

"Where are they going to sit? How much is the omnibus?" asks one girl.

"If you want to buy the bus, ours is not for sale."

"I want to pay for the ride! What are we waiting for anyway?"

"More passengers."

"Where will they sit?"

"There is space."

"We are late. We want to catch the only bus to Chirumanzu, *muzukuru*."

"And is that my fault? You were waiting for your daughter-in-law to make tea for you!"

"There is no more Buttercup, Stock Margarine and Lobels bread to go with your tea," interjects the driver.

"Gone, gone, gone, *ambuya*!"

"And that is my fault?"

"Next time you visit - we know they can't afford visiting you - bring mealie-meal, cow beans, dried beef and sheep fat and..."

"Firewood."

"Drinking water."

"They fetch some to bath in from the surrounding streams, including Mukuvisi River."

"T One, Copacabana, brother, get in."

"I have two rands and twenty-five cents."

"Let's go."

A gentleman with a designer suit enters and squats. There are no proper seats except a rise with an almost flat base directly above the engine of the omnibus. He sits facing all the other passengers except the two in the front seat. His phone rings.

"I will give back your money when I get it. I am in Victoria Falls right now. l will only be in Harare on Thursday," he disconnects the call and mumbles some inaudible curses.

"Is this your Victoria Falls, my son?" asks the golden girl.

"Mbuya, leave him alone. Do not harass my customers! What kind of person calls after a debt on a Monday morning anyway?"

"He should go to the Reserve Bank and ask them to convert his zillions to rands, pulas and dollars!" someone interjects.

"Who is not humiliated everyday anyway?"

"Yens."

"No, we don't want those people in our land!"

"There are already here and what will we do?"

"Those mean slave drivers!"

"My *muzukuru* who worked for them tells me that they give ten-minute lunches and they wait for you as you eat so you go back to work as soon as you're done. No day off, no leave!"

"In our land."

"In our sovereign land."

The man with the nice suit seems unsettled. He keeps on fidgeting, ignoring his phone which is ringing non-stop. His hands are sweating and shaking and a horde of conflicting sentiments show on his face. He tries to look out of the window to get some fresh air but cannot. His improvised seat is too low for comfort. The man looks like someone sitting on an alcove of death, on a voyage to a lost place. I forget my own grief and sympathise with him for a moment. Life is devouring me like that spider which devours its partner after mating, crunching him to a stain.

"Sure, that man is cruel. His wife is sick on her deathbed and he is busy arranging to marry her younger sister, whom he has already impregnated!" the golden girl who has been quiet all along complains to her friend.

"The younger sister is wrong. She was supposed to refuse his advances, and obviously she was not raped."

"Who says she was raped when she abandoned the children she came to help her sister with, and chose to help her brother-in-law with his sexual needs."

"He wants to marry her and formalise their adultery. I doubt the sister will survive if that happens."

"She says it is not her fault that the brother-in-law loves her. He is renting a beautiful house for her and he even bought her a new car."

"That sharp-tongued girl, wait and see. What goes around comes around. In the future, the same man will divorce her for somebody younger and more beautiful…"

"I will come back after a while. I could have stayed longer to nurse her. The problem is that my house could be a disaster. My husband's junior wife will cause all kinds of confusion and pain if she is left alone for too long in the village. I have to go and arrange things so I may come back with my heart settled."

"Get off my bus, parents. This is our destination."

"Hey, conductor, you promised you were going to Copacabana! How dare you short-change us?"

"It is not our fault. We cannot go that far. We can't risk having our windscreen broken by the police."

"You said Fourth Street! At least we could have planned our trips differently."

The answer came like a storm. "People of Zimbabwe, since when have you ever questioned anything unfair done to you? Are you trying to question me because you think that I am not educated? You welcome harassment and intimidation from those who sit at the top, burning your money and decency to ashes. I do not even have your change for your fare. We will meet on your way back. You have no cars of your own anyway so we will meet again later!"

There is no joy at the Fourth Street terminus. I am paired with a guy who has paid with a ten rand note. I have paid with a dollar note. We were given a dollar for change. I give up my 50 cents by buying a bottle of *maheu* energy drink that I do not need and pass the change to my waiting partner. Two women who are also paired refuse to compromise. The vendors are of no use as they ask them to buy something first before they can offer change.

"You buy something first so that we split the money between you."

"You buy, rather. I need the coin too, I have no other," complains the woman who had refused the token earlier.

"You can have it all. I no longer need the change. I will walk home. We used to walk anyway in 2005."

The other woman walks away triumphantly. I give her a dollar quietly and another elderly man gives her ten-pula in coins. A vendor gives her a bottle of *maheu* energy drink. A small crowd has gathered at the scene.

"This is Obama's money! It came with its own problems."

"I agree, *mufes. Zvakapresser.*"

"See this scar on my right eye? I was paired with a woman with a baby who refused to buy her crying baby some yoghurt with her change. I ended up buying some *sadza* with some chicken liver sauce for my lunch and that cost sixty-five cents. She fed her baby from my plate to consume the fifteen cents change. Whilst I was still enjoying the soup, in a twinkle of an eye, a hard blow stung me and sent me to the ground."

"Ha ha ha!"

"Ha ha ha!"

"The husband appeared from nowhere and punched me before wrestling me to the ground. If it was not for the security guard who had seen us quarrelling before, I would have been history by now."

"Oh, sorry, what do we do now?"

"Wait."

"For the rain?"

"I said to wait."

"For the coming of the Lord?"

"I said wait."

"For the money in the bank which I saved and banked?"

"I said wait quietly."

"Whilst my eyes swell with inflation?"

"I said do what you know best, wait."

"Other people are failing to manage their weight."

"Wait."

"I said wait in the manner of a pregnant woman, in silence. It is the noisy bird which gets a stone from the catapult. If toilets can wait to be flushed at seven-thirty in the evening, you can wait too. Wait."

Let Me Tell You

I was taking out muffins from the oven when I heard laughter from the study where my father sat with my daughter, Zamokuhle, and niece, Zenani. I tiptoed towards the passage and hid with my back against the wall, unashamed of my eavesdropping. The giggling continued.

"Let me tell you, you should always be on the lookout for potential drinkers of whisky. Not only that, consider also how they will drink it!"

"Khulu, that is impossible. How can you tell what a boy shall drink by the time he grows into a man?"

"Easy, let me tell you!"

There was more giggling from the girls.

My father was quite a character. He was loved as much as he was hated in the community. It did not take him a lot of effort to attract women, some who were as young as his grandchildren. It is said women were the reason he was excommunicated from the local Catholic Church by the priest, years before I was born. But did he care? He said he would rather wallow in paganism than worship at a church where the priest thought he was Christ himself. I was surprised when he was asked to give the eulogy at my cousin, Nomqhele's, funeral. Nomqhele had died of a combination of emotional abuse and the HIV-related illnesses back in the day when people referred to HIV only as "a short illness" or "a long illness". She was an actuarial scientist. She was often spotted sitting outside the huge company offices she worked for after 10pm, waiting for her husband to give her a lift home. The husband never allowed Nomqhele to buy her own car even when she could afford it. Even when Nomqhele's company offered her a car, the husband had advised her to send it back. He would have no wife who would be seen gallivanting around town on her own, he argued. My father had never got to know Nomqhele's man closely. He had quickly disapproved of him when he learnt the man had no basic O' level and actually wanted to marry Nomqhele. My father had been annoyed by the fact that where his sister, Nomqhele's mother, had been a nurse herself, Nomqhele was sinking very low.

As my father walked erect towards the podium at church, the thousand feet of the mourners could be heard shuffling in anxiety and uncertainty. Whispers filtered through the sombre atmosphere. He reached the podium and searched the crowds with his swift eyes before taking his handkerchief to wipe away his sweat mingled with tears. He gathered himself and spoke with so much force, it could have lifted the roof off the church.

"If I may ask all of you who call yourselves Nomqhele's relatives, why are you crying? I am asking you who lived in this town with her, why are you mourning?"

There was silence and wiping of eyes.

"You, my sister, you are a fool. Worst of all fools together with your husband... Fools cooked in fools' pots! You sat on your bums as you watched my niece get devoured by that illiterate hyena calling itself a man in broad daylight. Is that not so? Now you sit sniffling in here for what! Were there no men of her class who could have married your daughter had you helped her divorce the scumbag of a pig sitting over there among its wretched illiterate relatives who are all as ugly as sin? Even if she had not got married, would that have been a problem? She had a future. You, my relatives, who knew what she was going through and hid the information from me, I hate you! You talk about it now when she is all bones waiting for termites. You pig, when my sister gave my niece to you, was she written slave and punchbag on her forehead…?"

My aunt, his youngest sister, and my sister rose and walked him away from the podium, tears flowing from his eyes. After his outburst, the master of ceremonies was left speechless as he waited for calm to return amongst the mourners. The grieving from all who were there resembled that of the Zulus when Queen Nandi passed on. The difference was that some nodded with their faces hanging down. I was among those who smiled and cried at the same time. A few moments later, my father fell from his seat and was carried out of the church. We all knew it was fatigue from the night's vigil.

My father discouraged boys from talking to girls who "fried, baked and cooked their hair," accusing them of not knowing who they are and where they came from.

"Khulu, you have not told us how to separate real men

from the rest."

"They should take pride in men's matters. You need to check the books they read, that is if they read at all. Check which TV programs they watch and how long they stay watching television, what they do around the house and what they talk about!"

"Huh, Khulu!"

"Let me tell you, avoid those men who involve themselves in feminine activities! Those who move around the house waiting for their mothers to make porridge and bake cakes for them as they scratch their snort, don't give them a second glance!"

"He he he!" the girls responded.

"You are clever girls. You, Zamo, it is your final year at university, isn't it?"

"*Yebo*, Khulu, final year it is for me."

"You should bring that boyfriend of yours here. I will tell you what he is, what he will be in the future."

"He does not drink beer."

"I did not say that all men must drink beer. Of course, some men are pastors. Let me tell you something that you women don't know. You want men who do not drink but you won't like them especially if they don't have a special hobby which takes them away from the kitchen. Most men who don't drink are always on their women's cases. They notice every little mistake in the kitchen and house. In general, they are the worst in commanding girls and women, demanding all sorts, even from their churches! Above all they lack information!"

"Ah, Khulu!"

"I am just saying what I have observed."

My father graced village occasions in Italian designer suits, cycling on his bicycle, carrying a cooler box with his favourite single malt whisky and some ice blocks. He ate salads which he made himself from the vegetables he grew in his small garden next to the homestead. He roasted goat, lamb and beef from his own kraals and made smoked ham. He was the unofficial spokesperson for the Chief because of his good command of the Queen's language. He read anything and everything written in English.

What made me uncomfortable around him was sometimes he could be as vulgar as they come. There was no word which could not come from his mouth. He demanded to make a speech at my wedding. When I refused, he threatened not to attend the wedding at all. His opening words were advice to me that the only way to a man's heart was through his stomach, not through his testicles. That remained an unpleasant joke to my husband and I. My father was once banished from my brother's house for remarks and comments of that kind. He did not care about his daughter-in-law's threat. He still visited, claiming he was only visiting his grandchildren. He did not care whether that could cause my brother to lose his wife. My sister-in-law is a modern woman who wears wigs and could not survive a day without a helper. Her strength is in bringing money to their household which I think is fair. Her maids served her meals in bed. When she was not sleeping, she watched television from her bedroom and came out only when she visited her friends or went shopping. My father had commented in her presence that he would not be surprised if my brother changed his wife's sanitary pads. That was what earned him a red card.

My father's friends were reminded at every opportunity that there was no respectable profession that he did not produce from amongst his children and grandchildren, all from his meagre civil servant's salary. Speaking at my uncle's funeral the previous year and taking support from self-proclaimed Esquire cane, my father spoke, "Today my brother has gone to join our ancestors, without shame. It is all our way. What else can a man want when his family boasts of the best neuro-surgeon in the country that would be sought after by Cecil John Rhodes himself if he was still alive? Five general practitioners. I mean doctors, to those who don't understand English. We have a veterinary surgeon too and a dentist. We have a metallurgist, an aircraft engineer and recently, a pilot."

He paused and looked for his granddaughter who was a pilot. "I am sure each and every one of you would kill to have your sons and daughters join our family. Let me tell you, we do not welcome those who are illiterate as they can never be compatible with us. Besides, we don't want to be drawn back. Even if we are to be cursed with prostitutes in the family, they will be better prostitutes, educated ones..."

On that day it was his aunt who escorted him away and out of the tent. Some people were fascinated by such remarks and others were offended. The good thing is nobody left the funeral service or other previous events. I could not determine the reasons but just assumed it was out of the respect and sympathy they had for my mother who was a humble servant of the community.

"When I met your grandmother, there were things I looked for in a woman that I would marry and call my wife."

I heard the sound of ice dropping into glass followed by silence and I waited, curious too.

"What were they Khulu?"

"Let me tell you. I wanted a woman who loved herself and her environment. Who used her hands and brains more than her mouth and feet?"

"That is broad, Khulu, what do you mean?"

"Of course, she was a shy woman, always with a book or crocheting, knitting or plaiting her friend's hair!"

"Where and how did you meet her?"

"Wait!"

I tiptoed back to cover my muffins as I heard him walk towards the bathroom. Anticipation hung in the air. As soon as I heard him walk back, I returned to my position. My mind strayed as I remembered the day, he was slapped by Auntie Thembi for remarking that men must not think or behave like women who menstruate. I almost exposed myself, trying to muffle laughter. Auntie Thembi later confided in me that what made her do what she was regretting then was there was a new priest from our local Catholic Church. I laughed at her because I felt she had overreacted. The priest was going to get used to my father anyway with time. I teased her, saying that I felt that was not how educated people behaved.

"Your grandmother was such a difficult woman who made me realise this thing called love. She made me work mentally and emotionally before I could win her heart. A real challenge she was. She trained with my sister, the late Nomqhele's – may her soul rest in peace – mother and they stayed at the same nurse's home. I discovered her when I visited my sister but it still took me a few more weeks to be able talk to her. I bought your grandmother some presents that she refused to take and that oiled my determination. It took me a year after we started dating to get her to come to the room that I rented in Mzilikazi back then, in the sixties. It would have been easier for me to rob the bank of England than touch her skirts."

"Ha ha ha!"

"Yoh!"

"You see, there are very few or no such women at all these days, with these gadgets and social media. People boast of having friends they never met in real life. They talk of followers as if they were a religion! Nowadays they fall in love on social media!"

"Khulu!"

"Women and girls who send pictures of themselves in the nude to men."

There was silence from the girls.

"That is what you do!"

"Then what happened Khulu?"

"I pretended to be sick and she came, sat by my chair knitting and checking on my temperature from time to time. She cooked and fed me whilst I feigned pain. She did not wonder why her patient had such huge appetite!"

"The appetite had remained in the illness."

"Ha ha ha!"

"I was alright. After that she started visiting me after realising that I was a gentleman after all. Your grandmother never sat on her hands like you women of today. She cooked for me, washed my clothes as she still does today. Our bedroom is sacred and she cleaned it herself from the day I married her till today. Call me what you want but speaking as an African man, I believe that is what bonds our marriages and makes us respect our wives!"

"Things have changed, Khulu. During your days most men went to work to bring money home but these days both husbands and wives are employed."

"Let me tell you, women used to work even during the days of Tshaka. Actually, they did more work than men. Women worked around the home, raising children, cooking, making clothes for their families as it is written even in the Bible, in Proverbs 31!"

"Khulu, you are awesome!"

"Thank you, but I would not marry today's women because they use their hands only on the television remote, and for eating and scratching their bodies. They type on their phones all day long, even into the night!"

"Ha ha ha!"

"Things have changed Khulu!"

"That is indisputable, but if you want to live a full life, as if you are in heaven, like me, stick to what I have taught you!"

My father rode his bicycle following a footpath through the dense Mopane forest to the shops to drink and talk with his friends who were the learned of our community. He always wore nice clothes, golf shirts and designer shirts from the islands. He carried his cooler box with a bottle of whiskey and some ice. He had a ready audience; some being fascinated by his exposure to the world from his travelling and some maybe went for his freedom of speech. My father danced like Michael Jackson at the age of 78. He loved jazz too.

"Your mother grew up a clever girl and I knew she was not going to pick the wrong man for a husband..."

"And if she did?"

"If she did, I was going to chase the moron away from my house with a knobkerrie!"

"Ha ha ha!"

"Did you know that my father was going to be a drinker of whisky?"

"He passed the interview with merit!"

"What interview?"

"You are asking me that? How could he marry my daughter before I interviewed him?"

"Oh, my poor dad! He went through a lot of trouble with you to marry Mama!"

"Of course, but it was not trouble. I was simply protecting my daughter. I was looking out for her because she is not a cheap commodity!"

"Khulu ha, ne!"

"Ten heads of cattle he paid and he is good with my daughter, so I am a happy man! My heaven is here!" He paused to take a sip from his glass.

"Where is your dad now?" he glared at the girls.

"Italy. On business."

"You see, this is what I mean, not in Mbare-Musika, touting for passengers to Raffingora or Egodini queue, marshalling passengers to Beula-Nseula!"

"Ha ha ha!"

"Let me tell you, no poverty-stricken, leach-infested son of nobody could touch my girl, even over my dead body! I would have woken up and gone to the ruffian's parents to stop the wedding."

"Ha ha ha!" the girls laughed with their hearts. I waited

till their laughter got spent. He quietly poured himself more whisky. I could hear the ice bucket crackling as he fetched more ice.

"No nun-rapist could marry my daughter!"

"Khulu that is not fair. Love is blind!"

"You know what girls, you attract your own equal through what you do, your behaviour and where you go. Love with your heart but think with your head."

"That is impossible, Khulu. Love has nothing to do with reasoning"

"Oh! Ho ho ho! Let me tell you, it must."

I suppressed laughter as I thought of the day my husband first paid my father a visit. I was careful not to warn my lover as I wanted him to be himself. I was going to marry him whether my father approved or not. I met the man who became my husband when I was mature enough to know what I wanted and what was good for me. I knew they would get along because my father rated people according to their educational backgrounds and their family history. I found it so unfair.

My man was my father's opposite, very calm and collected. My man could listen for a whole decade without interrupting the speaker. My father did not only talk loudly, he also gesticulated and jumped up and down when it suited him. Most of my father's friends were young enough to be his sons, grandsons even. He was a man who celebrated life every day. He often reminded those who questioned his attitude towards life that he had endured everything by toiling every day in the fields, working for his family. He said he sweated, planning how he would supplement his civil servant's income so that he could pay all his children's fees up to university. There were ten of us including cousins and extended family. None of his children lived in a house without a swimming pool, a bar and study. He had flown and cruised on boats in the islands, went to Paris, rode on camels in the Middle East and even shopped at Harrods. Who, in the entire village would tell him a thing? He boasted that he had a life that most of the politicians could not even dream of. He often invited his friends over and would ask my mother to prepare English breakfast with the bacon that he kept frozen in the petrol-powered freezer that we bought for him in South Africa.

"This is not food for the white man only but for us too who can converse with him in his language, those who have crossed the oceans in planes and touched women in bikinis on the beaches of Zanzibar." He would say with his fork laden with a crispy slice of bacon on its way to his mouth.

My mother would go besides herself in shame and try to pacify the situation by changing the subject. He would start on something else which would chase her away from the breakfast table.

"When you eat this kind of food, you attract women like bees to nectar. If I did not ignore them, this house would be buzzing with children."

Then, as if he had not gone far already, he would start on a new wave, "I, as an African man, can marry as many women as I want. It is a custom. I am careful not to choose women as dark-skinned as I. Not that dark women are not beautiful. There are some dark-and-lovelies out there! But I want them fair-skinned, with long legs, big busts and not a single pimple on their faces. I want them smooth-skinned as ivory, ripe, pleasant and sweet smelling!" he said pretending not to notice the annoyance on my mother's face. We all knew that what annoyed her most was that she was dark in complexion and did not have a big bust.

His friends would fidget in discomfort knowing it was true to some extent. Always careful not to talk with food in his mouth, he would continue, "Overseas, there are clubs where I pay to watch them strip to nothing and dance around poles. I wonder when my daughter in California will send me a ticket so I can bring the second wife whom I met in Zurich."

"You have been saying that ever since you came back from America!" my mother would snap before taking the dishes out and disappearing to go do some chore or other.

"There is one in California and another in Switzerland but the one I met in Zurich is the best! She has everything, I mean everything." He stood to gesticulate in description of the woman's curves. His friends would sit there listening excitedly and eagerly waiting for him to bring a bottle of single malt whisky.

We often wondered with my sister when his women

hobby started. When we grew up, he was such a responsible father we loved. We never suspected anything like that happening. He was always home every weekend, worked in the fields and attended village developmental meetings with other men. His favourite hobby was reading. He read while resting in the shade of a tree or as he lay on his bed in the afternoon. We neither lacked nor were we ever sent away from school for non-payment of school fees. He taught the boys never to budget on their wives' salaries if they got married. That would make them less of men and they would never be fully respected by their wives.

"Your father, Zamo, is my favourite son-in-law… I do not mean in terms of money. I don't want his money. I never want anyone's money as you know I have enough of my own!"

"Khulu!" they exclaimed in unison.

"Yes, I have money! I mean enough money for me and for your grandmother to spend in the home. You can narrate this story to your father if you like. I just want a good life for me, for you and your mother, for everybody and the community at large, even for those illiterate oafs I try to educate everyday back in the village. Your father takes care of my daughter... they are good together! If your father was not good enough for my daughter, I was going to let your uncle, Zeni's father marry her instead!" he lifted his glass to his mouth.

"That is incest!"

"Let me tell you, I said if it was allowed by law of nature

and God Almighty! I would not want to create another Moab in Africa!"

"What happened in Moab?"

"You must read the holy book more, you, Zeni. It was Lot and his daughters who created the population of Moab."

Zeni's father was an agronomist. He had divorced Zeni's mother for her alcoholism.

"You see, girls. You must work towards inventing something! We want new things. George Eastman invented film, Thomas Edison invented light bulbs, Alexander Graham Bell invented the telephone you love so much, then talk about Einstein!"

"Oh my God! Khulu, how do you know all these things?"

"How silly of you to ask! It is written somewhere. By the way, these days you don't read. You sit typing on your phones the whole day even as you sit on your toilet seat, emptying your bowels!"

"Khulu!"

"You read only to pass your examinations."

There was silence from the girls.

"It is true, I am saying what I have seen and heard with my own ears which don't have plugs! You don't read, you just google things. Your English is atrocious. You can't speak your own languages fluently either! I don't even know where you belong!"

At my daughter's graduation ceremony, my father danced till all the youngsters moved away from the dance floor. He danced till he sweated wet. He danced to Harry Belafonte, Oliver Mtukudzi, Black Mambazo, R Kelly, Rihanna, Beyonce, Zahara and Mafikizolo. Days later, videos of his dancing were circulating on social media platforms. My husband filmed him even though he often said he did not want his life recorded. Every time I watched the video, I cried tears of both joy and loss.

When my father eventually died, one could not tell whether it was a funeral or a party. Men wore summer jeans and golf shirts, suits and hats dotting feathers on the side. Some carried canes and cooler boxes. Most men carried bottles of single malt whisky and drank sparingly from them like birds drinking water from ponds, speaking in rehearsed English sentences. Women wore brassieres stuffed to make their breasts look bigger, painted their faces to a lighter shade and wore different kinds of lipstick which made the priest, Father Zulu, smile before the service. When Uncle Melusi called to the mourners to bring any debts or if there was a woman with children fathered by my father to come forward, we were surprised to see that there were none, despite the rumours. He, however, read a letter written by my father that a local school mistress was to be given a head of five cattle or cash equivalent for keeping him good company, warm and happy. There was sadness and longing though, judging from people's eyes. The Chief appeared devastated and lost. People danced, imitating my father's jives and moves. Behind the granary, at the makeshift funeral kitchen, at the graveyard it was all, "Let me tell you.

The Prisoner

"Shut up! Everyone in here, shut up!"

Everyone turned to look at the man who had been sitting with his friend quietly throughout the day. The older man was startled too by his companion's sudden remarks. Dr Nomonde looked at the professor who had his gaze studiously on the man.

"You, what do you know about being married? Do you have a wife? Don't you have things better suited to your age to talk about?"

"Does your wife beat you?" mocked the bespectacled youth from the backseat.

"Shut up! Another word and you will find yourself going out through this window!"

"That is rather out of proportion. What did the boys do? These are just general discussions to while away time."

"Shut up, you whore!"

The dreadlocked lady was stunned to be called a whore by a stranger, a man for that matter. She looked at the man without saying a word, studying his demeanour. Her temperament seemed to sympathise with him. One of the men who had spent the day with her stood up, fists folded, ready for blows.

"Who are you calling a whore?" he charged at him.

"Why didn't you stop all the discussions before? What is

so special about this one?"

"If your wife abuses you, it is not our fault. Let the boys free, they are providing the entertainment we need at this moment!"

"I said shut up or I will kill someone. Let me be," the angry man answered in defiance.

"Who is holding you?"

"Face your demons alone!"

"I will kill someone here, now." The angry man stamped the floor of the bus so hard it shook. Two more men stood to face him. The man looked down and started sobbing. His old friend went close to him and said something to the two men who then retreated to their seats.

Overlapping flashes of lighting rent the darkness on the west. The cracks of thunder that followed shook the bus. A seething cascade of water made a thin mist as it hit hot surfaces. Everything else whined and creaked in the wind and only the tower lights did not go off.

The miserable man's life started playing in his mind like a movie. He wondered if there was anyone who ever married an eternally dissatisfied and controlling wife as his. He wanted to get to South Africa in a second, work for a few months and then proceed to Dubai, farther and farther away from her. He thought of finding a healer who could cleanse him from her spells first in case she wormed her way back into his life.

Mandla had worked with the friend he was travelling with

for an engineering firm in Bulawayo for the past twenty years. After their firm finally sold its last asset, they decided to cross the border as everyone was doing. They had left Bulawayo for Harare to get their fast-track passports en-route to Cape Town together. The incident and closure of the firm propelled Mandla to make his decision to start afresh in life.

As calm returned to the youths and other passengers on the bus, Mandla recollected an incident which had happened six months before the factory closed. He had gone to assist his colleague who had hit a pothole along Khami Road, ending up with two worn out tyres and a bent rim. As he went up the staircase back to his office, he had been called by the secretary to rush to his office. His wife was on the phone. Sweat trickled down his spine. The phone rang three times before he could pick it up.

"Hello?"

"She is in the country, isn't she?"

"Good afternoon, Mrs Ndlovu," he greeted his scold and martinet of a wife whom an army with all its sledge machines could not have prised out of his life. He had been fully shattered by his wife's nagging that even if he was with his friends, he felt agitated.

"Do not good afternoon me! She is in the country?"

"Vimbiso! Who is in the country?"

"Oh! So, I am now a fool? If you play games with me, I am going to the papers right now. She is going to be stripped of her prestigious job before I sue her for every cent. She will die a pauper. You were with her; that is why you were not answering your cell phone and you have been out of the office for two hours!"

"I left my cell phone charging since we had no power last night. I was out of the office to assist someone along Khami Road. I do not know what you are talking about!"

"You better come home now and explain yourself!"

"I will come at lunch time when I bring the children back from school."

"I said now, Mandla!"

"Vimbiso, I have work to do. You are the one who makes endless demands. Besides, I am coming two hours from now. I have work to do!"

"I said now! The newspaper people are only a call away and their paper will sell with my story!"

Mandla could still hear her panting after she had hung up. He thought for a while and decided to check if Rose was indeed in town. Her answering machine told him that Rose had gone to her country. She would be back in Geneva, Switzerland in two weeks. Mandla was stunned. How did his wife know Rose's number? He scratched his head and decided he had no fuel to waste. Knowing his wife's lunatic tendencies, he decided to drop everything and go to her before her insecurities drove her to do something he would later regret. He remembered when he had ignored her and was called by the police after she had visited and kidnapped Rose's child from her flat. It was Rose's understanding that had her set free. He stood up and descended the stairs. His mind was so congested that he did not see Mdara Ndoro coming up the stairs as he walked out.

"Hey *mfana wami*! Why do you look like you are going to a funeral?"

"I am going to my funeral, that woman is killing me with her insecurities!" Mandla said, thinking of how often he had intervened between Vimbiso and his mother.

"Women…" Mdara Ndoro answered thoughtfully. "Go and sort it out. We will talk later!"

Seething with anger, Mandla waved as he rushed out of the building and paused before putting the keys into the ignition. He moved his body with much effort into the car. He did not want Rose to be in any trouble. He felt guilty that he had exposed her to it. He was on separation, pending divorce, when he met Rose at a business meeting in Victoria Falls and after presenting a paper together, they fell in love. Mandla felt God had answered his prayers by giving him the woman he must have married in the first place. Rose refused to have Mandla marry her before she was sure that his divorce went through. Vimbiso, who knew that the little love she had for him would pale to nothing alongside Rose's, stole all his professional certificates, their investment files and gave them to her mother. She refused to sign the divorce papers brought to her by the lawyer. She also stole and edited, for legal effects, the pictures Mandla and Rose took together on a Cruise Ship on the Zambezi River on the day of the business symposium. The pictures became tools for blackmail which helped her back into Mandla's life before she started threatening Rose as well. Rose subsequently ended the relationship with Mandla because he could not explain what was happening.

Mandla loved Rose. He was almost obsessed with her but Rose stood her ground. He lived with Vimbiso who knew he was indeed fed up with her. During the period that Vimbiso was fighting with Mandla, she fell pregnant and had their second child in January, another in December of the same year and the following year in October. She had enough reinforcements to help her cling to Mandla who still did not give up on Rose. Even if Vimbiso knew Rose did not want to get married to Mandla, she was not convinced that the tussle was over.

Mandla still called Rose, secretly following her on her other dates and tracing her suitors to lie to them that he and Rose were married. Vimbiso searched Mandla's phone and found Rose's numbers. Threats ensued. When Vimbiso read about Rose in the newspapers, she would throw tantrums for weeks. If she had the chance, she would make Rose's mother swallow her daughter back into her womb. Mandla and his wife remained a pain in Rose's life until Rose was saved by the diplomatic post she got to Geneva.

Rose was happy to leave the country with her son. She was happy to be far away from Mandla and his lunatic wife. Vimbiso thought it was her medicine that had driven Rose away, so each time Rose visited, she was threatened beyond limits. She owned Bulawayo and Rose was not to be seen near it.

Mandla's stomach churned as he neared home. His business partner and ever-present companion, fear, almost tore him apart as he turned his car into his road in Hillside. Vimbiso's moods determined his. She complained about everything. If she was not shouting at her two maids, then it was at him or the children. When she was moody, he coiled on his side of the bed until she woke him for conjugal rights. Whatever mood she was in, she was always aflame with sexual desires which he could never extinguish. Rose was always a headline in their house. A lever to torment Mandla and cover up Vimbiso's own issues. When she was drunk, Vimbiso became violent, hurling abusive and vulgar words at everyone in the vicinity. Mandla hid some of the incidents from his friends and family but they knew, although they failed to save him. Vimbiso's hands were used to eat, scratch, and depress her television remote and her cellular phone, tracking Mandla's movements or talking to her friends who were just like her.

Mandla provided for his family no matter how big it grew. Vimbiso lived to issue orders to her two maids who did everything for her, including making her bed and bringing her breakfast in bed. One maid had beaten her before fleeing and the other had written her a letter to remind her how lucky she was to live off a husband she did not deserve. The maid promised in the letter that she would be back for the husband. She would show Mandla peace outside hell. Vimbiso had read the letter with horror. She let everybody read it, hoping for sympathy.

Rose too, who had been approvingly namechecked in the famous letter, was to hear of it.

Mandla parked his car as his wife came out of the house, ready to spit venom. Her two indispensable maids were hanging her bed linen on the washing line, constantly throwing inquisitive glances at their madam whom they had heard screaming on the phone earlier. The girls felt sorry for Mandla. His relatives, having since stopped visiting, then came, feigning happiness for fear that Vimbiso would poison their son. They did not know that she could never do such a thing. How would he have provided for her and slept with her every night, with or without his love, from the grave?

He had stopped to buy flowers to calm the storm but the hands that were supposed to receive them visited his cheek with a slap. The girls momentarily stopped what they were doing, startled. Mandla walked sheepishly to their bedroom which was usually their courtroom.

"Deny it, she is in town!"

"I do not know if Rose is in town. Besides, this is her country of birth."

"Now you defend her?" she answered with a tiger shark smile.

"Defend her? This is her country and she has her family

here. If she is here, is it a problem?"

"Oh, yes. It is a problem when whores are around to destroy people's marriages. She destroyed hers and now she wants my children to grow up without a father!"

"Rose is not a whore. She did not destroy her marriage, she divorced properly because she had married a clingy and useless husband. It is high time you knew that not all single women are immoral women. She is the one who decided to divorce her lazy and dangerously insecure husband who is just like you. She could not have made a better decision. I applaud her from my heart. Just think of what she has taken quietly from you all these years. I am tired of this, Vimbiso! Tell me what you called me here for, so that I may go back to work!"

"We are going together and I will drive the car. I am going to take you and the kids to work and school every day and pick you up after work at 5pm. I will also punish you. I will have to punish you. You will make love to me again every morning, no matter what! Now, let's go!"

"Vimbiso, you are mad! Do you know that I may not have a salary again this month? Where will the fuel for all those trips come from?"

"You are a man, you will make a plan."

Mandla had run a professional eye on her and looked at her resignedly. He walked out of the house quickly and waited for her in the car. She came and drove him to work without saying a word. At the office, Mandla lay in the rest chair in his office, thinking of the mistake he had made by marrying Vimbiso.

They had met at university when Mandla studied mechanical engineering and Vimbiso, agriculture, which she never finished after failing the examinations. She then dropped out of college and worked as a receptionist with the intention of enrolling at a nursing school later, but never did. Mandla picked laziness and silent controlling traits in her and started going back on his promise to marry her. He started dating another girl who was studying medicine. When Vimbiso found out, she cried buckets in Mandla's office before verbally and physically attacking the girl, claiming she was already pregnant with Mandla's child. The student doctor dumped him after the incident. Vimbiso cried herself pale until Mandla's friends advised him to take her back. She had eloped and fallen pregnant before Mandla could reorient himself. Vimbiso's parents demanded lobola and a wedding. Her problems had surfaced more fiercely than before. They lived in separation until he met Rose.

Mandla decided to phone Angie, Rose's friend.

"Oh, your wife who thinks she became holy by getting married to you has traced her. Please, leave Rose alone. She has had more than enough from you both!"

"So, she is in town?"

"Mandla, listen, you are the one with a problem. Please, leave Rose out of your miserable life. Now that you have called me from your cell phone, I am going to endure nightmares from your wife whose business is to track Rose. Please, Mandla, let us be!"

"Leave Vimbiso to me. I will handle her!"

"Don't be silly, Mandla. Who does not know she has her finger wrapped around your neck? Since when have you ever risen above her as a man? You have just watched her humiliate Rose since the very day you came into her life. You went on to show us that you still loved each other by having three children in three years. Go and love each other at home!"

"Angie, don't say that to me. Who says having children is a sign of love? I am forced to live with Vimbiso by circumstances. If she wants to have ten children, she will. She is the woman and is in control. It is complicated, Angie. I will commit suicide if I cannot be with Rose. Where is she?"

"Mandla, please! If you love Rose, you will leave her alone. You seem to forget the parcel she received in her letter box? Do you still remember the threats written on a piece of paper, the lion's teeth, the herbs and the bottle with a strange liquid and Rose's picture in it?"

"That does not work. Even if it worked and Rose died, was it going to make me love her? I have kids at home and I am just being dutiful. I do not love Vimbiso and she knows it!"

"Then go and tell Vimbiso that. I do not care who you love or don't love."

"You know that I love Rose, alive or dead!"

"Mandla, don't be thick-headed. Maybe you are also

blinded by muti. It is not about Rose being alive or dead. She needs peace and space from you and your wife. You both seem confused. Do not talk about love with Vimbiso. She knows you are just being dutiful in everything you do and you do not love her. She wants you to work for her and look after the children. You are a good father – everybody knows you are. She just wants to fix Rose!"

"Vimbiso is haunted by her inadequacies. The only thing she knows is to wait for me in bed. There is nothing else she does for me. Where is Rose?"

"She is at her parents' home, preparing for her wedding at a private ceremony tomorrow, somewhere around Zimbabwe. At least she is free at last. Enjoy your life with Vimbiso, dear Mandla!"

Mandla felt like tonnes of stone had fallen on him. Angie's tone had a serious air he could not brush aside. It had been a year since Rose answered his calls. He thought of the incident with the lion's teeth which Vimbiso was seen placing on Rose's gate. Rose survived all Vimbiso's scheming and witch spells. Mandla knew his wife wore a uniform to church but had a cunning and cruel heart. She had spent all her life trying to destroy Rose. Mandla felt sorry for Rose and a great pain because of losing her.

He had called his relatives one morning after discovering another pack of herbs, animal and snake skins with Rose's name in them and declarations that she should die a pauper or go mad. Mandla's relatives, who were also tired of

Vimbiso, drove two cars to Murehwa to her people to return her but the Ndlovu family was turned away with their wife. They said a wife was only returned for infidelity not witchcraft. Vimbiso was happy to return, singing her favourite song, "I am not going anywhere." Rose remained a victim as much as Mandla. There he was, stuck with Vimbiso for life.

As passengers in the bus debated on wives' issues, he had seen a vivid procession of Vimbiso's words and actions over the past twenty years that they were married. Many times, he had thought of running away to hide in the rocky crevices of Ematojeni. The thought of her gave him the agony of a knife blade twisted in his heart. Vimbiso had ruled his existence in pain and nagging. He had never had peaceful sleep unless he was away on a business call. Now that there was no chance with Rose, he was prepared to join the ever-hurrying Johannesburg people who moved as if they had heard a wisp of a diamond or gold claim on a reef somewhere. He thought of Cecil John Rhodes's men rushing to get King Lobengula to sign treaties. He waited with their patience in the bus as did Rhodes's men who waited two seasons to get an audience from the king outside his kraal, koBulawayo, a century and some decades ago.

My Grandfather's Kraal

We walked in a single file to the village well in the morning wind, holding our water barrels by our elbows. The sun had not risen from its mother's breast. Smoke from the household fires filled the air after filtering through the Mopane tree leaves which were everywhere. The path meandered and crossed other smaller paths all over the village. Everybody else in the village was yet to wake up except my grandfather, the grandmothers, the mothers and us the girls. Grandfather was always the first soul to wake up, his first stop being the cattle kraal where he passed water. The singing of pestles on mortars could be heard from a neighbouring village. The sounds came from two or three groups of women pounding from the same mortar, clapping, chatting and laughing away. The women must have been pounding sprouted rapoko grains to be used for fermenting the beer they were brewing for *ilima* which was to be held in two days. Other echoes announcing the peaceful start of the day were heard from everywhere. Women washed their faces in cold water and then cleaned their mouths and teeth with charcoal.

Sibahle and Nothabo led the way, Dudu and I following grudgingly behind. We did not like being woken up before dawn. It was a school holiday and there was not a lot of work since it was neither the planting nor the harvesting season.

The dry season had lain to waste the countryside. Field gates were kept open for livestock to feed on whatever they desired. Cattle fed on the dried maize stalks first, then the finger millet, the sorghum and lastly, the grass. Goats fancied legume leaves more. Donkeys rushed to the melons and the grass. The sheep nibbled on everything quietly.

We passed some cross-roads and saw a broken earthen pot, broken pieces of a water guard, some ashes and a bundle of herbs thrown on top of the fresh heap. Someone had performed some ritual at night because the stuff had not been there the previous evening. We each spit three times on our left shoulders as an absolution.

In the mornings, Gogo MaSibiya nursed her frequent hangover from her beer drinking binges, her snores rising with the sun. She would sometimes shout at her daughters-in- law for waking her up for breakfast. Grandfather did not drink alcohol. Gogo Sibiya often came home alone at night, unafraid of the dark, as I did myself. We would often hear her from a distance singing an old village ditty:

Kwaze kwamnandi,
kwamnandi,
kwamnandi,
Ye, ye, ye,
kwaze kwamnandi
ezweni.

Life was good for my grandmother whose duty it was to complain about the curse of having lazy daughters-in-law. As we neared the well, we saw Zodwa, coming from the opposite direction with her maternal aunt, Thembi. She had been married the previous month to a man from their tribe. I wondered if she had already finished her new bridal duties, some of which included collecting firewood every morning with a thin cloth strapped across her chest. She did not have the cloth on.

One after the other, we all enquired after Zodwa's health before turning to greet her with splashes of water we scooped from our water barrels. We giggled as she ducked and used her barrel to hide from the cold liquid.

"I am well, if you are well too, my industrious girls. By the way, what did you say the name of your little sister with the ten-litre gallon was?" she directed the question to Sibahle while pointing at me.

"Bumbekile."

I forced a shy smile at her. I was not happy that she asked other people about me when I was neither deaf nor dumb. Sibahle stole a glance at me, maybe surprised at my response. I was a very quiet and shy girl but never allowed anybody to violate or look down on me. She removed the logs which were arranged to make a gate. Nothabo also stole a glance at me. I sucked my right thumb to conceal my discomfort. She secretly knew I was bound to feel that way with that kind of attention. I preferred not to be noticed, all the time.

“Do the boys know yet?” Zodwa asked Nothabo.

“Yes, we are meeting in the afternoon when they have gathered and secured the cattle in the kraals. You should be ready with your brothers. We have decided the best time would be after supper,” Nothabo smiled, winking at Zodwa.

I was afraid of water, so I was never allowed into the well. When Marabi River flooded, blocking us from going to and coming home from school, mother and Mlamleli often had a tough time helping me across. I would shake and shiver at the sight of the flooding waters carrying everything with them. Often, I would lift my little feet, avoiding contact with the sand and debris which tickled my feet. I did not trust the sensation caused by sand moving underneath my feet. It felt as if the earth was disintegrating and flowing with the water.

Sibahle and Zodwa helped each other lift the water barrels outside, placing them on a flat rise created from soil scooped from the well to deepen it and open more underground fountains and springs. We used the same gritty soil to scrub our pots to remove the stubborn black soot. Aunty Thembi made *inkatha* for us, soft pads of cloth wound together, coiled and then flattened, to put on our heads, to soften the loads of our barrels. She also promised to come by in the afternoon to plait my hair and Dudu’s. From the well, we walked abreast where the path was wide enough as we competed to walk the longest distance without holding our barrel with our hands. We sang our favourite ditties as we walked, swaying this way and that rhythmically.

"*Gogo, golani amacimbi*"

"*Liwabambe liwachaye*"

"*Limnandi icimbi lephane*!"

"*Limnandi emsileni*"

"Sibahle and Nothabo tell me so that I can start sharpening my…"

"Hoes and sickles, MaMlotshwa! Whoever volunteered that information to you has cooked us in a fools' pot!" Nothabo complained. I had not seen her approach.

"Anyway, since this is still a family affair, you will only know when your time comes, now how did you wake up?" Sibahle enquired.

It was neither hoeing season nor was there a grass cutting ceremony for thatching. The grass had all been devoured by the livestock who ruled the fields at the time.

"So, what am I if I am not family? Tell me I want to know!" she asked, feigning anger. Sibahle had understood Nothabo's wink.

"By the way, you are a baboon which is known for harvesting unripe berries." We all laughed at Nothabo's remark.

"Just tell me now. Have you asked him yet?"

As soon as we got home, we put our water barrels down and rushed off to collect firewood. As we walked back home, the sun appended its flames on us save for our heads which were protected from it by our heavy loads of firewood. As it was at its zenith, it shortened our shadows, making them fall directly at our feet. I walked on stubs of grass, avoiding the hot, sandy, loamy soils made loose by our frequent traffic and that of the livestock on the path. We had to make time too for plaiting our hair, an activity which was considered a luxury by mother.

When we got home, we sat for lunch that mother had prepared.

"Ha! MaMkhwebu, today the sun is taking fish out of water!"

"Bumbekile, bring MaMlotshwa a goatskin mat before she collapses from dehydration."

I doubted MaMlotshwa would collapse from the heat. She was as fat as she was tall. She was ever moving from village to village in the sun, heat, rain or cold. She slept very late and woke before the third cockerel announced the approach of a new day. I felt she would do better as a village preacher. As soon as I gave her the mat, she put it near mother and washed her hands in the dirty water which had been used by Thethelela to wash his muddy hands. I offered to get her clean water from the earthen pot in the kitchen but she refused and dug her hand into the steaming hot *isitshwala* that mother was sharing with Mamncane MaMkandla.

In no time, they had swept clean their relish plates. MaMlotshwa turned her neck towards Nothabo and asked her to bring a gourd of fermented milk from the kitchen. MaMkandla motioned for her to stop as she proceeded to Gogo MaSibiya's kitchen to get a small earthen pot which still contained the dried pumpkin leaves in peanut butter sauce from the previous supper. MaMlotshwa did not wait for her to sit down. She received the pot and ladled the sauce into their plate, licking her fingers in the process. Mother ate quietly but Mamncane MaMkandla stopped eating, for a while and then stood up and disappeared behind Gogo's granary.

"It is the pregnancy, never mind her. She shall deliver soon," mother said, softly. I thought MaMlotshwa would feel piqued with the consequences of her lousy, unhygienic traits.

"Bumbi, tell her she will give birth to a child who looks like me, with this kind of hatred." MaMlotshwa spoke with food dancing in her open mouth whilst she polished the traces of the remaining sauce left in the earthen pot.

"We do not want our baby to look like you. What would we do with those drum noses of yours!" teased Nothabo. "She will look like her mother if she is a girl."

I smiled, wishing the same. Mamncane MaMkandla was beautiful in every sense. I called her dark and lovely.

"When I was your age, every time I passed, men broke their necks trying to get a glimpse of me, eh, *uyadlala wena*! My waistline was that of a wasp. My legs were as smooth as a bottle, my stomach so flat one wouldn't think a baby could grow in it!" She said all these with a small morsel of *isitshwala* stuck on her little finger.

Mamncane MaMkandla came back after we had finished eating and cleared the dishes. Nobody asked her questions as mother boiled some herbs in a disused tin which had originally contained sun jam. MaMkandla drank the medicine slowly, without frowning and fell asleep on a reed mat.

Mother stood up and tightened her waist wrapper which revealed her ageless curves before disappearing into her bedroom hut without saying anything. She never let the afternoon go by without doing anything. She worked patiently with her needles, sometimes sewing new clothes, mending torn ones or even darning. She crocheted and studded her patterns with big needles. These days she often knitted baby clothes for our new baby that Mamncane MaMkandla was expecting. I quietly washed the dishes in the shade.

"I had come to spend the day waiting here with you," MaMlotshwa said to Nothabo in a supposed whisper.

"Right now, I am waiting for Mamncane Thembi who is coming to plait Bumbi and Dudu's hair. We have to make another trip to the well before we pound finger millet for supper."

"Do not avoid my question!"

"MaMlotshwa, please, do not let mother hear us. Please, do not scandalise me and leave me to it."

"Her moon is which one?"

"She is two moons away from her expected month of delivery."

"The load is becoming heavier and demanding, I see."

Our dog Thatha started barking ferociously. I had just

finished washing the dishes and placed them on the wooden stand to dry. I started to run towards the main gate to investigate, but tripped on one of the poles supporting the stand and almost fell. All the dishes fell one after the other to the ground but I did not mind. I ran towards the screaming pair. The previous week, Thatha had bitten an old woman who had come to complain that our goats had forced themselves into her well and drank all the water. There had been a lot of trouble after the incident.

Before I got to the gate, I saw Zodwa and Mamncane Thembi leaping into the boys' bedroom hut. Zodwa had flattened herself on her stomach under the single bed whilst Mamncane Thembi held strong the door which was threatening to fall apart from Thatha's pressure from outside. He was jumping up and down, scratching on the door with his claws, standing on his hind legs. In that state it was only I who could manage him when the boys were not there as it was.

"Thatha, stop it at once!"

Immediately, he stopped barking, tail between his legs and walked towards me slowly, as if he was about to apologise. We were very good friends with Thatha who was often my bodyguard in the bush when Mlamleli and Nkosiyabo took me hunting. I must have been five years old when we started hunting together. They would carry me when I got tired. When I slept, they lay me in the shades of the trees lining the river on the vast sands which made good bedding for my small fragile body. Thatha would stay to watch over me, barking at whatever animal or reptile that came near our sanctuary, all day long. When I woke up, I would stay at the same place until the boys came for me, sometimes at sunset. When they delayed, Thatha would lead me home safely.

"Sorry Mamncane, please stay inside until Mother and Nothabo come for you. Do not worry, it won't bite you," I warned them as I led Thatha towards the dish stand to feed him whilst I put back the fallen plates.

Mother and Nothabo welcomed the visitors and ushered them to where we had been sitting. Mother had already organised another goat skin mat for Zodwa and a reed mat for Mamncane Thembi.

Nothabo brought wool from mother's bedroom hut and gave it to Mamncane Thembi who had started parting my hair to plait it.

"Thembi, your sister said to me you were getting married last month. Are you not supposed to be a *malokazana* now? What are you doing here?" MaMlotshwa enquired not long after.

Thembi stopped plaiting me and asked me to stretch my feet because I had been sitting in one position for too long. We strolled towards the Mbondo tree outside the yard where Khulu sat making hoe handles with my brothers. They had just arrived from the bush where they had gone to cut the logs required for the job.

"Have you eaten anything today, Bu?"

"Yes, Khulu, why do you ask?" I giggled.

"Go with Dudu to my hut and bring the gourd of *umcaba* you will find under my table. Bring the duiker biltong. Bring all of it."

"Yes, Khulu," we said as we ran towards his hut. After the fire had smouldered and had enough charcoal, Khulu put the biltong directly on the charcoal and let it roast. He then removed the roasted biltong and gave me a big portion. I ate a little and gave some to Dudu who had registered her dissatisfaction through her fidgeting and pouting. We chewed in silence, savouring the taste of the wild meat. Khulu then scooped *umcaba* with a wooden spoon into our cupped hands. We ate the filling meal in silence.

After Mamncane Thembi finished plaiting our hair, we went to bath with Gogo Sibiya at the communal village well. We had just started bathing when we heard people talking.

"Yes, they will ask him this evening after the arrival of the boys," someone said in a hushed tone from the well. I could not immediately identify the voice.

I lathered soap on my towel and soaped my body, enjoying the smooth feel of the bubbles. Our bathroom was an open space behind the well, between large rocks in the middle of the opening of shrubs which protected us from possible onlookers. We scrubbed our feet on the rocks. There was no mud to be worried about as the area had little stones holding the surface together. If swept together and collected, the stones would do well as three quarter stones for builders. We enjoyed the warm bath; our water having been warmed by the sun.

Gogo Sibiya loved scrubbing herself with rough stones first before lathering. She would roll black, snaky fragments of dirt, which increased as she scrubbed away. The dirt came out to expose her light skin. That would have made a good show had there been some voyeurs nearby. I chatted and laughed with Gogo Sibiya a lot especially when there were no strangers near us. She told me a lot of stories and taught me traditional etiquette. The person I did not feel comfortable with was not always there, my father. He worked in Bulawayo at some factory where blankets were made, not Egoli where most of my friend's fathers dug for the white man's gold.

"Thembi ran away from the husband before the marriage even started!" MaMlotshwa loudly confided in someone.

"Why?" asked another voice I could not hear clearly.

"*Nholo wemizana* ..."

"She ran away on the first night of the marriage!"

"You tell me that till this day, they still do that cave ritual? She did well and I would have done the same. How did she escape?"

Gogo banged her zinc dish she had been bathing in to deter us from hearing the details. I could still hear the conversation in pieces as MaMlotshwa did not quickly understand her warning. Gogo Sibiya finally gave up banging her dish.

"Thembi says, on the evening of the first day she arrived at her husband's place, as she took her bath, Buhe's father undressed and lay on the newly married couple's matrimonial bed. Thembi, sensing that the story her friend had told her was about to happen to her, wore her dirty clothes and disappeared in the thick darkness. She ran throughout the night to her parents' homestead. She arrived in the early hours of the morning. Her mother told her to go to her aunts instead. That was tradition. Buhe's father was supposed to sleep with her first. Buhe had already paid half his lobola, including some live beasts. Buhe then followed Thembi and promised to sort out the matter, but Thembi said she would rather go and find a job, pay him back and forget about the doomed marriage. Her father does not even know she is here; he could have sent her brothers to take her to her husband's people!" There was some silence from the woman who was listening.

"If it was me, daughter of Mlotshwa, I would have pulled his old thing and given it to the dogs! What do they think women are?"

I thought about the question the rest of the afternoon.

We gathered *ekhutheni* after supper, twenty-two of us, grandchildren of Khulu Mahlangu, known as Godonga, his totem name. According to tradition, all his female children and grandchildren would be called MaGodongas. We sat chatting and giggling away, waiting for the right time to put across our request.

"I must be someone special to have all of you caring to come and chat the night away with me," teased Khulu.

"We always want to but most of the times we will be helping our mothers with chores," replied Zodwa.

"Khulu is just joking with you. This is not a place for women," Thethelela said carelessly, knocking his tiny feet in the air, lying on his back on Sibahle's lap.

"See who will give you porridge tomorrow!" Sibahle warned.

"You don't even cook well!" her brother mocked her again.

"*Hawu!* Gogo MaGodonga, my father's aunt! You still haven't mastered the pot. Do not worry, you take after MaSibiya whom I taught to make porridge when I married her," Khulu said.

"MaSibiya… what? You are a good for nothing old man who teaches his grandchildren nothing but mischief. One day you will pay a full herd of cattle as a fine at the chief's court!" MaSibiya who had just arrived answered, almost in a murmur, as she removed the sickles, hoe stubs and the blunt knives she had stuck on the grass thatch in front of the hut which stood alone in the centre of the homestead.

"And whose grave are you visiting tonight with your friends as we all snore away?" Khulu retaliated.

"*Oa umhu*, daughter of Sibiya who lies quietly in Transvaal!"

Gogo mumbled. Khulu started humming his favourite song.

Kudala kwakunganje,
Umhlabu 'yaphenduka!
Kwakubusa uMambo loMzilikazi!
Sawela kuTshangana
Saguqa ngamadolo
Inkosi uLobhengula yasinyamalala

We all joined in and sang harmoniously. Birds also sang their nocturnal hymns. Stars shone brightly, supporting the moonlight. Crickets and whatever else made noises in the veld and fields nearby whilst cows mooed for their calves in the nearby kraals. Calves bellowed for their mothers too in the nearby goat kraals where they were closed in. Lambs cried for their mothers' fine tits in their little kraals. Somewhere, a drunk sang an old village ditty in a drunken stupor as he staggered home.

In rehearsed tones, we started on our request.

"Khulu Mahlangu, Godonga baba, we have come again in humility us your grandchildren…" We paused.

"I am all ears; let it all come out of your hearts my grandchildren, before the witches snatch it out. I can see the light is still on in one of their friend's hut." His joke diffused the tension as we continued after laughter.

"The request touches on your most treasured investment, Khulu Godonga," it was Mlamleli who continued alone as we all collected ourselves anxiously.

"What is my most treasured investment?"

"Your kraal."

"Oh, do you even have to ask to build our kraal? You are all naughty children, bringing your sisters here for men's matters!"

Khulu's sarcasm amputated our hopes, at least mine. No one said anything. There was only Thethelela's fidgeting because of the anxiety that had kept him awake that late.

The following morning, we woke up with our eyes smarting as we sang our favourite hymns, sweeping the yard in a row, Nothabo, Mamncane MaMkandla and I. We swept with some brooms we made from some grass which grew in the fields. We started from behind the granaries, making small heaps as we went along. We collected the rubbish in wheelbarrows and went to empty them in the rubbish pits. After sweeping, we went to fetch water to wash the entrails of the huge beast that was to be slaughtered.

We had gone twice when we saw a group of clansmen standing together around the kraal. Mlamleli sharpened the axe on a stone and Nkosiyabo cut branches of Mophane trees. Thethelela and Dudu's brother pulled them to the kraal where Jamluthi the ox stood tied to a msusu tree at the centre of the kraal. Nkosiyabo was placing huge logs in the fire that somebody I could not recognise was building. Khulu stood talking to MaMlothswa's husband who was going to strike down the beast.

The distant sound of a screaming baby broke the morning excitement and tranquillity. Wails from an elderly woman followed. Some feminine voice consoled the wailer. The sound of the worn-out axle of a moving wheelbarrow mixed with all the wailing and consoling.

"*Maye e, maye e*...! Even if my father chases me away, I will go and find a job."

"We are home now, MaGodonga, nobody will chase you away. We all love you. Keep quiet, now or you will scare everyone here. Be strong like a woman."

That was clearly MaMlotshwa's voice. We put our water barrels down and stood still. Instinct denied us the strength to go to the well. All the men put their tools down too. We all gazed in the direction of the approaching voices. The party then appeared in full view. We were all astounded. In the wheelbarrow sat Aunty Sithini, my father's youngest sister. Her hand was tied with a sling to her neck. So swollen was it that it was almost the size of her torso. She wore no head wrapper. Cakes of dry blood had hardened on her kinky hair; trickles of fresh blood still flowed from the two wounds on her head. Her blouse was torn to shreds. A wound was visible above her breast. She sat in the wheelbarrow with her left leg placed on the top of the front of the vehicle. Her right eye was shiny from swelling; trickles of dry blood laced the skin on her cheek. She wore a petticoat which was also soaked in blood and dust.

MaMlotshwa quickly covered her legs as men came closer to investigate. Her daughter stopped crying.

After much consolation, Aunty Sithini stopped crying and then it became our turn to cry. I took the baby from

MaMlotshwa. Nkosiyabo carried the toddler home. Mamncane MaMkandla carried all our empty water barrels. Khulu followed silently at a slight distance, hands behind his back.

MaMlotshwa and Gogo Sibiya helped each other wash aunt Sithini's wounds. Mother fed her thin porridge mixed with herbs. After that, she could only steal a few hours of sleep and wake up from the excruciating pain until mother gave her some painkillers. Irritation and anger were finally overcome by fatigue. Her groans seemed enormous in the silence of the torrid afternoon, bandages clinging to her body like bodysuits. Her hair had been shaved clean by mother who had bandaged the wounds carefully in her infinite patience.

Almost everybody spent the day at home as the atmosphere had sobered itself. The intensity of everybody's anger had put the craving of meat to sleep.

Jamluthi had been let free and led to join the other cattle.

Everybody went to sleep early that night.

A man called and repeated his calling-and-greeting. He was behind the wooden logs drawn together to make the security boundary of the homestead, so one could not see him from inside.

Mamncane MaMkandla had asked me to show her the tree with the bark suitable for medicine to wash aunty Sithini's wounds.

"Eh, eGodonga! Father of my father, baba, eMahlangu."

Silence.

We stood there deciding whether to call Khulu or wake the boys. As I neared the boys hut, I could hear them talking from the interior of the hut.

"It is him! Bring a spear and a knobkerrie, Mlamleli," whispered Nkosiyabo. In a flash Nkosiyabo and Mlamleli dashed to the gate with raised spears and knobkerries. Tshebukani Ncube, Aunt Sithini's husband, leaned on his back to the wall as he crouched, unaware, gazing at us. Mlamleli hit him on his chest with a knobkerrie and he staggered backwards and fell. As he tried to rise and run away, Nkosiyabo threw a spear which missed him by a whisker as he dived and stood on one leg, the other caught between two boundary logs. The spear struck the log and remained there. The man remained rooted to the ground. "Today we will help you see your ancestors, son of a witch! You will wish your mother never brought you to this earth."

Nkosiyabo hit him hard with a knobkerrie and we went round in circles, blood spraying out from the wound on his head. Mlamleli removed the spear from where it was stuck, ran backwards in reverse and from a distance, raised his spear at close range, ready to strike. Mamncane MaMkandla let out a loud scream and fainted. Thethelela screamed. Chickens quaked. Thatha barked ferociously. War seemed to be everywhere at once.

"Stop it right now! Stop. I do not want blood on my hands. What do you think you are doing, Mlamleli hii!"

Khulu shouted, running towards the scene.

Nothabo brought a bucket of cold water which they poured on Mamncane MaMkandla. Nothing happened. Mother sent me for a broken clay pot piece with red-hot charcoals. Gogo Sibiya brought some powdered herbs and sprinkled them on top of the embers. A choking smell rose with the little laces of clouds. They passed the smoke near her nostrils. She inhaled, shook a bit and sneezed. She then slowly opened her eyes.

Tshebukani was made to sit alone in the girls' bedroom hut all day long. Mother sent Nothabo and Sibahle with breakfast, lunch and dinner which they ate themselves and falsely reported to mother that Tshebukani said thank you very much. The following day, as the elders deliberated on the solution, the girls ate all his meals again, leaving him only water to drink.

The meeting between the two clans was set for the third day at sunset. That day there was chicken stew for lunch which the girls ate as he watched. His feet had been tied by Nothabo and Sibahle secretly. They cursed him, quietly telling him how foolish he was to spit out the morsel of fortune that his ancestors had placed on his hands by giving him Aunty Sithini as a wife.

That afternoon, Khulu and Mother joined other villagers to help a neighbour mend his field with Mopane branches, *ilima*. As soon as they left, MaMlotshwa appeared from nowhere and started singing a war song. Nothabo, Sibahle,

Zodwa, Mlamleli and Nkosiyabo locked aunt Sithini in her hut. They then beat the unsuspecting Tshebukani with huge sticks. They descended on him like hungry leopards, MaMlotshwa cheering and dancing to the ordeal. They had agreed that talking to Tshebukani and letting him go would be like curing a disease that was never seen before with common herbs. He squirmed, mourned and hissed like a snake. He mellowed like a cow and quaked like a duck, as MaMlotshwa danced, clapped and ululated. He screamed like a sow in a slaughterhouse. They polished the job off by beating the soles of his feet with a black rubber. It was after he had emptied his bowels with premature stool that they left him for a while in an obscene position. The girls then gave him some water to bath and Nkosiyabo gave him his own pair of trousers and a clean shirt.

I was ordered to make tea for him, horrified as l was.

Apart from Khulu and MaMlotshwa, no other adult knew what had transpired during that day.

Two grown men and an old woman from Tshebukani Ncube's clan sat in the shade of a timeless *guwe* tree the following afternoon. MaMlotshwa and her husband Dube, could not be left out. Mahlangu men and those affiliated with them sat on stools whilst the Ncube clan sat with women on reed mats, in a bow-like order. They could not be allowed the luxury of sitting on stools, not with the criminal case facing them. Everyone's emotions were at fever pitch.

Ncube's brother whose job, MaMlotshwa had told us,

involved licking plates for the Boers in the suburbs of Johannesburg, sat with his knee lifted from the ground, supported by his interlocked fingers. He too had brought nothing from those kitchens except a funny accent, a shining yellow shirt and a pair of red and green trousers, which his wife washed whilst he waited for them to dry. He also had his hat which had a feather flying about, off a leather band tied to its brim. His sitting position only mounted the irritation and anger of his in-laws. He was reprimanded by Khulu's sister, Gogo MaGodonga who also reminded him that he was not in one of his drinking spots in the night clubs of eGoli. We often fled on Gogo MaGodonga's approach as her temper was as fierce as that of an angry bull. When she spoke, she cut without drawing blood. Her character could also be likened to a rat's gnawing, biting and soothing.

Aunty Sithini was helped outside by Gogo Lindelwe who, though quiet, was not some soup which one could lick in a hurry. No matter how angry she was, her words carried gaiety and never her anger. Those to whom she was unknown saw an ewe of a person. She did not relish to see siblings fighting openly, arguing that when such happens, strangers always reaped their harvest.

Tshebukani Ncube was brought to the meeting place by Mlamleli and Nkosiyabo who helped aid his snail's pace by supporting his sides, much to the amazement of everyone, excluding Khulu. He sat so stiff; he might have been made of stone. He sat near his sister who had toes which were as widespread as a duck's.

Red dust spewed at them from a passing whirlwind, blowing away old women's skirts. The heat remained even as the sun was going down.

"We are not going to waste each other's time as we can all see that it has already been eaten by the cat. I would like to ask my in-laws if they have any married daughters in their clan?" my uncle opened the talks after the greetings.

"Son, do not waste our time. Go straight to the point! Who cares if they ever raised marriageable daughters?" Khulu interjected from his favourite position on his stool with his back against the trunk of the *guwe* tree.

"What had your wife done to deserve that kind of beating…?"

"Brother, your question implies that women are supposed to be beaten. Let me ask them, why did you try to kill our daughter?" MaMlotshwa asked, making jingling sounds with the dozen fetish bracelets she wore on her arms.

"Ahem, ahem," murmured the Ncube family. "You answer the question my brother," the frail woman surrendered the question back to her brother.

They debated back and forth until their faces started swimming in the orange waters of the setting sun. Aunty was to stay with us until her body returned to her, probably after two months. The husband was to come every day to dig up tree stubs from Mamncane MaMkandla's new field. He was also ordered to pay a ram and a goat to be slaughtered for relish during the period of their stay.

Daily chores established themselves again. Grandfather opened his kraal after a month and ordered another heifer to be slaughtered for us instead. As soon as Aunty Sithini got better, we woke up one day to discover she had gone back to her husband before the family's agreed time.

Uncle Njabulo's Return

Besides a quick step, colourful clothes, a bicycle fitted with shiny decorations and a funny accent, Uncle Njabulo brought nothing for his wife and children when he returned. He had left fifteen years before to dig for gold for the white man in Randburg, South Africa, eGoli. He had an album and a towel which he always hung around his neck. He came in August, unexpected. I did not know him. I had only heard from mother that I had an uncle far away, down South.

Uncle Njabulo alighted from Phelandaba bus at Malaba Store, at the Nyashongwe Primary School bus stop, carrying a briefcase and a travelling bag with one hand, the other pushing his bicycle. He wore a shiny red shirt, a pair of tight black jeans, *ubhokati* and a pair of pointed crocodile skin shoes which were clearly an imitation. A thin striped tie dangled from his neck all the way past his imitation leather waist belt. He rarely ever removed his tie even when he cycled to the shops. When he did, he replaced it with an equally bright-coloured scarf. Two double-vent blazers and a hat with a feather on the side were also his trademark. The day he alighted from the bus; he wore a grey blazer. It was mid-afternoon when the bus arrived. It was a sports day.

He walked with the children who had finished their sporting activities. Two boys offered to carry his bags as he cycled slowly alongside them, chatting. The children enjoyed his accent and that made him talk more, asking them about people they did not know. He expanded like a balloon with pride. From the bus stop, they descended to the west, past the borehole pumped by a windmill on their left and crossed Simpathe River. He got off the bicycle when a slight boy offered to push it for him. He moved as if he was afraid the abundant sands on the riverbed would fill up his shoes. The tall, thin boy whose shorts were still torn after numerous coloured patches were sewn onto them, one on top of the other, gave Uncle back his bicycle as they neared the riverbank. The boy walked barefoot with the rest. His skin showed signs of malnutrition, his hair had an orange tinge and his heels were cracked. Even though most children walked barefoot, they dangled Tenderfoot canvas shoes on their necks. The boy had none. He was as unbothered as his friends were.

The road meandered and stretched. It twisted and turned as they passed through the new village crèche on the right, a new homestead and a new field on the left. A herd of cattle loitered ahead. He hooted his bicycle bell, much to the delight and amusement of his young fans who jeered excitedly.

The girls walked abreast behind them. He twitched his shoulders often and wiped his brow with the towel dangling off his neck. The paths parted and a group of children went the other way. Uncle Njabulo cycled on with the remaining boys carrying his bags. They passed two homesteads abreast of each other across the path. Even though he wished people would notice him, nobody did as there was a thick hedge of Mopane trees between the homesteads. Ahead, across a small stream, they could hear the sound of an axe cutting away wood for the fireplace or for some leafy branches to fence off the fields. The rainy season was approaching. If one did not protect the fields, goats and cattle would have free reign on newly germinated finger millet or groundnuts.

The boys could not see Khulu Dlodlo but they could tell it was him by the sound of his axe. Uncle Njabulo had left when his first child and son Bokani was two, and his wife was expecting a second child. The village headman had just allocated them some space to clear for a field after they had built their homestead the previous year. The new homestead had two thatched huts, a granary and a goat pen.

The sound of the axe grew louder. It was inevitable they were going to meet the chopper. The visitor was eager to be noticed by people, and his gaze darted back and forth. The old man stopped chopping and drew near the path to meet them.

"*Sawubona, mkhulu,*" Uncle Njabulo said, stretching out his hand. The old man stretched out his own wrinkled, chapped hand to meet the visitor's.

"*Yebo, ndodana,*" he answered, squinting, looking for familiar features on the younger man's face. He could not recognise him.

"You seem to have forgotten me, Baba Dlodlo. I am your

son, Njabulo," he told him with empty pride.

"Njabulo, eh, Njabulo., from which family? Age has taken its toll on your father here. My eyesight is waning now."

"Njabulo Ncube. I am the son of your neighbour, Thuthani, from his second wife, MaTshuma."

"Ah, ah, ah! You have just arrived from Jwansbek! I am happy you came after such a long time."

"All is well down there, we are doing extremely fine, yah, extremely fine. How is Mama MaMpunzi?"

"Oh, you did not hear about it? She passed away ten years ago." The old man felt the embarrassed look on Njabulo's face and quickly changed the subject.

The children had left the two adults talking and waited ahead, at some distance. The girls had been quickly swallowed by the thickness of the foliage.

"Did you recognise your son? He is grown up now!"

"My son, eh, which one is he, my Chief?" he stammered as he fiddled with his knuckles.

The old man lowered his chin in sorrow and called back Bokani who came trotting. Uncle Njabulo remained trapped in his own ridicule as the thin boy with tattered clothes waited for the old man to say what he had called him for. The old man wrestled with a series of thoughts, wondering if it was his position to perform the shameful exercise of introducing father and son. He lifted his axe and caressed its sharp end as if it were the breast of a young woman. He lifted his eyes slightly, covering the sun's rays with his palm as if pleading to it to help him. He coughed harshly and spit the phlegm across the path. His words were soft and carefully selected as he stammered the introduction.

"Bokani, my grandson, if you met your father along the path, would you recognise him?"

The boy only managed a confused smile. At his age, he had simply forgotten how he would relate to somebody called a father. All his friends' fathers came home at Christmas or Easter. If they did not, they sent new clothes, groceries and sweets, some of which his friends gave to him on their way to church. He and his sister Hanani had since stopped asking their mother to write to their father as her letters were never replied. They had also stopped passing messages with each passing aeroplane, to tell their father to come home and bring them sweets.

Uncle Njabulo stood as if seeking a stray thought. Bokani only managed to answer by shaking his head.

"Bokani, my grandson, this is your father. Njabulo, this is your boy. He is a very responsible young man. The mother could not have made it till this time without him."

"It shows he is a real Malaba, our blood yes, real blood. We are not as weak as women like other clans, *amahole*. You have grown my boy, time flies. How many goats do I have now?" he muttered unashamedly with sudden impulses.

"We have thirteen," stammered Bokani with fear, embarrassment, anger, and excitement all rolled in his chest. A lot of thoughts crossed his mind. *Who was this man who suddenly came to their life and claimed their goats?* He hated him at once. *Was his mother going to receive him with love? How about Hanani?* The boy held his anger as he walked away in silence, tears trickling down his flaccid cheeks.

Senzeni sat alone in her kitchen hut where she had made a fire to boil dried cow bean leaves for supper. She was thinking of cooking them in peanut butter sauce. Almost every day, they had sugar beans or dry bulgur, the closest they came to eating rice. The food was their allocation from a Catholic Church relief programme which fed the impoverished of the communities. She got the share after the community had agreed to register her as a widow. Senzeni had endured years of loneliness, struggle, throbbing fears and anxiety. Often, she had thought life would have been better if she was educated. If she had the chance, she would have gone back to school, even night school. She might become a nurse, a teacher or a doctor. She knew one woman doctor stationed at Mtshelanyemba Hospital. Those thoughts often made her as light as a leaf. The only dress she wore to church was handed down to her by her cousin, who was a nurse and trained at Brunapeg Mission Hospital. She had no shoes even to cover her feet from the cold during winter. Sometimes, she only managed to buy shoes for her children during winter with the money she got from selling pigs or roosters. She shared her two thin blankets with her children.

Her husband had written to her once, a year after he had

left, and the letter had two pictures enclosed. In the first of the pictures, he sat on a high stool, wearing a suit and a hat with a feather on the side. He sat with his foot resting on the rung and the other on the blue carpet. He was grinning into the camera, his dark lips revealing a chip of his gold tooth. In the other picture, he sat in the company of two women, both holding his shoulders, smiling mischievously. Nobody managed to identify the women within the whole of Thuthani's clan. It was clear they were not relatives. His smile stayed smeared on his face. His children knew him from those two pictures. Senzeni and the children had survived his agonising absence from their lives. She did not know what she would do if he suddenly came back.

Senzeni stood up from where she sat near the three stone hearth and wiped her eyebrows. She stood still, thinking of getting groundnuts from the granary to shell and pound for the peanut butter sauce. She rekindled the dying fire and went outside to get more firewood which she added to the fire. She blew on it, kneeling on the dung plastered floor of her kitchen hut. When she was sure the fire would not die, she took a reed basket and made for the granary to get the groundnuts. When she came back, she sat down to shell the groundnuts, contemplating brewing beer for the village men to help her close the open gaps on her field fence ahead of the rains. Only the sound of cracking groundnuts could be heard from outside her kitchen hut. It was a quiet afternoon. The earthen pot with dried vegetables made a swishing sound as hot air escaped from the improvised lid of another pot.

Njabulo's face kept surfacing on her mind. Every time his vision came, she tried to conceal it by humming her favourite hymn from church. Her right eye twitched and her right hand itched. She spit on the hand and smiled. Her cousin had promised to visit her from Brunapeg Mission. Every time Njabulo's image flashed, she tried to think of her sister who had promised her old kitchen utensils since she was moving to further her nursing career in the United Kingdom. She might even give her blankets and clothes, who knew, with the ways of the Lord! The vision made her angry as it persisted. She stood at once to pour the water which had been warming up in an Olivine tin placed on the side of the hearth, into the dried vegetables. She wondered about Bokani and Hanani's delay from school and then remembered that it was a sports day.

Senzeni had never been anywhere; her feet only knew the sandy loam soils of Mbome where she grew up. She had travelled only twice to Maphisa and Khezi to try and organise birth certificates for her children, to no avail. The father of the children was required to sign some forms. Her children existed unregistered like wild animals. This hurt Senzeni greatly. She wanted her children to be educated and have better lives than hers. Bokani could not write his exams to qualify for secondary school education because of the missing papers. He had repeated his grade twice, her attempt to keep him in school and out of mischief. Hanani was always top of her class. She loved books, and she read anything and everything written. Her teacher often gave her more material for reading. Her mind was overactive, it needed curtailing.

Njabulo was a lump of sin in Senzeni's heart as well as in his mother's womb. She sat alone thinking of her days as a young girl when Njabulo used to wait for her by Simukhwe River where she fetched water with other girls. He was her first lover and boyfriend. She had longed to nestle in his arms back then, when she had emotions of another kind. They would suck sweet and sour *mswantsha* fruits, picking wildflowers by the banks of the river as he made points into her heart. Life was good then. She had tasted the succulence of his love as their hearts flew together like mutable flights of doves. She loved him then and thought their love would last a lifetime. She would look at her hands which were as rough as an alligator's back. Then Njabulo would hold them quietly and forever. Their breaths were to flow together when they married.

She remembered for the longest time, breath by breath, the day he came for her with his alluring voice. On the night, even in the dark, Senzeni remembered his promising stride and his certain step. She had loved and trusted him. He had given her some coins to place under her reed mat as a sign to her parents that she had eloped with him. She did not care that he did not have money and was not employed. His love for her was enough. Njabulo would know all her being the following morning.

Now, as she sat alone, she did not know if she still loved him or not. Her body had longed to be touched by him, love unfulfilled. She could not compete with women in his album. They were beautiful, with soft, silky skins. She knew her role as a wife was to keep his home intact, his fields tilled and his livestock safely closed in their pens and kraals at night, safe from hyenas. MaKhuphe had been patient like a mantis, for a decade and a half, despite her agnatic status in the family. What would she do if he came? Who was he, even to the children? It had been too long even to rekindle the old love. Now she loved her children and found comfort in them.

Senzeni went outside and took a bucket of dirty water to the pigs which were now making angry growls from their pen. She felt bad as she hurried to them, not caring about the dirty splashes onto her skirt. The bow stood on its hind legs as she approached. Before she finished pouring water into the wooden troughs carved from a *safice* tree, the bow forced its mouth into the tin, spilling water on its face, and on Senzeni's already dirty skirts. She decided to go back and get clean water from the earthen beer pots in her kitchen. They were good for keeping her water cool. She met Hanani at the gate carrying a used packet full of salty cicadas.

"How has been your day, Mama?"

"It was fine, my dear, only it is too hot today. Where is Bokani?"

"They are helping a certain man who alighted from the

bus carry his bags. I left them talking with Khulu Dlodlo near the fields."

"You do not know the man they were helping?"

"I have never seen him before. He seems to be coming from South Africa, from his accent. He is also wearing very nice clothes."

"Did Khulu Dlodlo know him?"

"He seemed not to, but that was the time I left them talking and introducing each other."

Senzeni's heart leaped a bit with that statement but again, she did not know the reason. They entered the kitchen silently. Hanani rushed to get water to drink from the earthen pots. She ignored the water in the plastic bucket near the kitchen mud display on the wall. She then went to change from her tattered uniform into her home rags. MaKhuphe went back to the pig's pen with cool water after adding more wood to the fire and more water into the pot. Hanani came back and dished herself a fair share of *umxhanxa*, leaving some in the pot for Bokani.

As Senzeni entered the little gate at the side of their homestead she saw Bokani and his friend approaching, carrying luggage, and a stranger cycling along on his bicycle. She went into her kitchen hut without saying a word to Hanani. She felt a bit restless but surrendered the feeling to fatigue and heat. She bent by the hearth and opened the lid of the pot to feel if the vegetables were done. Satisfied, she took the pot down and replaced it with the water tin. She then took the three-legged pot outside to scrape off the cakes of thick porridge which had dried on the sides of the inside of the pot. She decided to go back to the kitchen to get warm water to pour into the pot to soften it. She regretted that she had forgotten to pour water in it the previous night. To make matters worse, it was finger millet *isitshwala*. Senzeni was startled to see the stranger outside her kitchen, so was Hanani. The stranger's nose resembled Bokani's.

"Sawubona MaKhu," Uncle Njabulo extended his hand to greet her. She was petrified to note it was her husband from his voice. Senzeni remained silent as words failed to come out of her mouth. Hanani held on to her mother's skirt, not understanding the situation.

"MaKhuphe, you do not recognise me. It is I, your husband, Njabulo." He removed his hat to reveal his nicely done hair, with a decorative line on the side. His pitch-black hair was parted to show a clean scalp underneath. Senzeni took a deep breath and extended her hand to greet him. She went into the kitchen to get a wooden stool and a goat skin mat. Hanani's eyes moved from her mother to the stranger with nervous frequency.

"Is this Hanani? Come and greet me. She takes so much after my sister, Dudu," he said, tapping his fingers on the thighs.

"It is her. She will be fourteen this September," Senzeni said with blood singing from her thumping heart. She waited for him to introduce himself to his children. Silence. Roaring rage. Sparks flew in her head. She took a deep breath. For once Njabulo's body stilled with cowardice; his heart went faint with fear.

"Bokani, go and call Gogo. Tell her we have a visitor and she must come now."

Their grandmother's homestead being a stone's throw away, Bokani ran without saying a word. All the while, Njabulo was nearly strangled by his fear, fear of the unknown. Hanani remained confused as she coiled herself near her mother. Senzeni felt she would let her mother-in-law, who also had as much heart as a dirt-eating toad, do the introductions. Njabulo fiddled with his hands. Senzeni stood up to remove the tin from the hearth. His eyes followed her behind. She was now thin, as thin as hunger and troubles make a woman. What was left was her old voluminous apron. The skin behind her legs was wrinkled and cracked and the soles of her feet left prints on the sandy soils of Mbome communal lands. Some cracks were bleeding. The pinafore she wore was so dirty even without the recent splashes of the pig's water. The hair under her headscarf resembled a mop. She and her children had last bathed with soap three weeks before. There was not much to do in the village which could earn her money. Since Uncle Njabulo had returned, maybe things were going to be better.

"Oh *maye…e…e*! Is this my child? *Mayee*, Njabulo, why do this to your family? I never thought I would see you alive, my child. Look at your children! Were you not thinking about them all along? Njabulo, my child!"

Gogo MaTshuma wailed with tears of joy and sorrow.

Njabulo looked down in embarrassment.

"We buried your father, your grandfather, your grandmother, your two nephews and your niece. Did you not hear of their deaths, my child?"

Gogo MaTshuma's wails rankled Senzeni as Uncle Njabulo looked at his shoes, motionless. Bokani remained still. The anxiety had repressed the hunger he felt as he walked from school before the drama had unfolded in his ears and eyes.

In no time, the whole clan had gathered at their homestead. Senzeni had deliberately left his bags untouched for his family to see what he had brought his children. Everybody was relieved and happy to see him except for Senzeni whose mind and emotions wreaked havoc as she prepared finger millet *isitshwala* and dried cow beans in peanut butter sauce.

"I do not eat this dark pap; isn't there something better?" the visitor complained at supper time, much to the amazement of everyone.

"This is what we have. We cannot afford meat if that is what you want." Senzeni was clearly annoyed.

"There are chickens I saw around, and Bokani told me I have thirteen goats now. You could slaughter a cockerel to welcome me if you were happy that I came. I do not eat this kind of pap! Try something better for me, woman!"

"Give her what you brought. She will cook for you in no time. Where would she get the delicacies when she is struggling to raise the children alone? I am sure you did not come to torment someone's daughter, my son. The children do not know you, and at least you could have waited for the introductions before blowing up like that. All these years you haven't even grown. Oh, please!" his mother clapped her hands once and raised her weary palm to show the number of years he had been away.

"I do not eat this type of food," he said again, pushing away the plates with his feet.

"Umh! You were bewitched by the dead, *mtanami*," Gogo MaTshuma spoke into his words which nobody seemed to understand.

"*Ngumuzi wami lo! Angibuswa ngumfazi*. This is my home. I shall not be ruled by a woman who came from her people with nothing but torn skirts stuck on her bones!"

"Njabulo my son, are you possessed? Surely, we need a cleansing ceremony!"

"Tomorrow morning, I am going to get some refined mealie meal and rice that she will cook for me. I do not eat *kak*. I will also slaughter the biggest goat from my kraal," boasted Uncle Njabulo.

"You do not have any goats in the kraal that you can think of slaughtering. Those are all my goats. The four goats you left in the kraal I sold to buy blankets for the children and pay the men who thatched the huts and mended the fields.

There are four goats in the kraal that are MaTshuma's and the other nine are mine which I bought with the money I earned from brewing beer and taking part in women's clubs," Senzeni said calmly.

"This is my home, and I am saying it again. I own everything here. You did not bring anything here from your people save for your tattered clothes. See if I am not going to do it!"

"My child, Njabulo, this is the first day you have set foot here after fifteen years, I repeat, fifteen years, and the first time your children have known you. Can't you at least try and maintain the peace you have found here." For a moment, Gogo MaTshuma thought her son was indeed bewitched.

As MaTshuma remonstrated with her son, Senzeni poured water into a metal twenty litre bucket and went behind the granary to bath, her warm tears adding to the water. She had to think about the future of her children, starting with having their births registered. The children sat quietly, waiting for their father to give them sweets and maybe new clothes from his bags to no avail. He had not brought bread even, which was normally brought by people who went to the local stores. Hanani gave up on him and instead cleared the dishes to wash them outside near the wooden table. When she finished, she and Bokani mixed the dirty water with finger millet chaff and then went to feed the pigs. Bokani had since gathered the goats and closed them in their kraal after separating the young ones from their mothers.

More trouble came at bedtime. Where was Uncle Njabulo going to sleep? He had no bed, no blankets, just his clothes and a palate for good food. Senzeni made bedding for the children in the kitchen hut with the blankets they normally shared.

"Mama, may you please lend us blankets for your son to sleep on?" Senzeni asked her mother-in-law.

"You mean there are no blankets here? You said you sold my goats to buy blankets. Where are those blankets now?" Uncle Njabulo demanded.

"We sold those goats fifteen years ago, before Hanani was born. Blankets do not last fifteen years with children weeing on them every night!" Ever calm and collected, Senzeni explained.

"Not to worry. Now that you are here you will take care of your family," his brother, Mthelisi, commented after a long silence.

"Bokani and Hanani, let's go and get Auntie Dudu's blankets for your father to sleep on," said MaTshuma as she stood to leave. "Sleep well, my children. I will not be coming back with the blankets."

"Sleep well too, mother," Mthelisi, his wife, and Senzeni replied in unison.

Uncle Mthelisi remained chatting with his brother as everybody else left to sleep. Senzeni accompanied her sister-in-law to seek some wise counsel on how to handle her husband. When she came back, Senzeni went to her bedroom hut to do what needed to be arranged. She had finally taken her husband's luggage to the bedroom.

"Gogo, is that our real father?" Hanani asked as they walked.

"Yes, *mzukulu* that is your real father. He left for South Africa before you were born."

"Why did he go to South Africa?"

"To look for a job."

"Did he find the job?"

"Of course, Hanani, do not be silly! How do you think he had been surviving there without a job?" Bokani answered with much annoyance.

"How far is South Africa from here, Gogo?" asked Hanani, confused.

"It does not matter how far it is. How come Motini' s father comes every Christmas and Easter, with new clothes and shoes for his children? He even takes them to the Trade Fair, yet he does not even wear those fancy clothes. Motini's brother, Themba, learns at Embakwe Mission. Not a single day was he sent away for non-payment of school fees," complained Bokani, stamping his feet.

"I do not like his attitude. I would prefer he stays there forever. It is better here with our mother and our hunger," lamented Hanani, almost in tears.

"If he is really my father, I would do much better without him too!"

"He is…"

"Enough of it, children! He is your father, and you still need to respect him," Gogo MaTshuma rebuked them.

"What is there to be respected about him? Swag, but no blankets to sleep in? Ha-a? I am better off without a father!"

The biggest goat was slaughtered in the morning despite Senzeni's protests. Uncle Njabulo had breakfast of fried liver and tea. Some sugar was borrowed from Uncle Mthelisi's wife, MaMkandla. Before the sun had ascended into the sky, Uncle Njabulo was cycling off to St Joseph's Business Centre. He sported a red shirt, striped black trousers, white pointed shoes, a grey double-vent jacket and a scarf on his neck. The feathered hat gave him shade and style. He made sure everybody noticed him along the way. He did not even feel that a lot of women scowled and howled at him for his lack of responsibility for his children. He never forgot his album wherever he went, to show off his lovely company of women and the beautiful places he had been with them. He boasted of being a ladies man.

He bought a ten-kilogramme packet of refined mealie-meal, rice, tomato and chilli sauce and a packet of potatoes. He said his wife and children would do very well with the finger millet *isitshwala* that they were used to whilst he enjoyed his refined foods. When the goat meat was finished, he commanded his wife to slaughter a chicken for him every two days. Senzeni did not only borrow a big dish for him to bath in but also a pair of clean sheets from Auntie Dudu's things. He claimed her blankets caused him some skin rash. For the whole fortnight he was home, he never entered the fields. In the week following Uncle Njabulo's return, Senzeni brewed traditional beer for the village men to help fence off the fields ahead of the rainy season. She woke up on the crowing of the second crow on the first day of beer brewing to light the huge fire which she would use to boil the drums of water. By dawn, the water was already boiling and she had done most of the primary work.

Uncle Njabulo's spit bubbles burst through the corners of his mouth as he lay breathing through it, making horrible sounds from the small windows of the bedroom hut. He was sleeping on the floor on a reed mat and the undulating sounds of his snores sometimes sounded like the murmur of men around a village fire exchanging a calabash of the fine brew. Little did Senzeni know that Uncle Njabulo had almost been beaten to a pulp the previous night at a bottle store at St Joseph's Business Centre. Had it not been for Uncle Mthelisi's interventions, Uncle Njabulo could have suffered a broken limb. In a drunken stupor, Uncle Njabulo had tried to kiss the school head's wife. It was the other drunkards who beat him up, not the headmaster himself.

Senzeni sat in brooding silence. She had finished taking out boiling water from the drums to mix with fermented corn mealie in large beer pots built into the back of her kitchen. It was a strenuous task, but what could she do? She unknotted her head scarf to let fresh air cool her body as well as her emotions. It was eight o'clock in the morning and the atmosphere was dehydrating as it was already burning hot. She then sat as inflexible as the railway tracks, her mind struggling with indecision. Should she leave, take her children to her mother, go for a job herself *to eGoli?* How about the children's birth certificates? Njabulo had disposed of his and was now a South African born in Mnambithi, KwaZulu Natal, as Bhekimpilo Mahlaba. Suddenly an idea shot with the impact of a bullet in her mind. Uncle Mthelisi. She would ask Uncle Mthelisi to bring the idea to Njabulo after breakfast when Njabulo was in a better mood. She felt better with that thought but then went back into her crabby self. Njabulo's ruthlessness and selfishness were stronger than her struggles. She regretted having waited for him as if he was going to bring her a tremendous gift. She tried to stand up but failed, all her limbs throbbing from fatigue. She had been lifting those twenty litre buckets with boiling water alone. The previous day, she had been carrying the same water from the well, two kilometres away, the whole morning and evening. This was after a week of pounding the sprouted maize, rapoko and sorghum to make fermented corn meal for the beer brewing. There was her husband also who wanted to be taken care of like a baby.

Strange sounds broke from Uncle Njabulo's snores from the bedroom hut, from his cracked lips which were held together by dried blood. He sounded like someone crying in a strong nasal trap. He was then awoken by the sun's rays which went through the small windows which were too small to fit a day-old baby's head. He had thought he dreamt of wood smoke.

"MaKhuphe where are you?" he called with a throttled voice.

Senzeni decided she would not answer him.

"Woman! I am calling you! When will you learn to show some respect? By the way, you women understand only the way of the knobkerrie!"

Senzeni eyed him but did not answer. Her outburst of emotion ebbed away with one sweeping gaze as she noticed his swollen face, the blue eye. There was also blood on his clothes.

"What happened? Where?" she asked in shock.

"Don't ask me questions, woman. Bring me warm water in a bucket. I want to bath now!" he barked at her, snarling like a bitch.

Over the top of her precipitous incline, her mind had stalled. An uncanny sensation of speed and danger swept across her mind and she moved back, feeling helpless. There was no point in asking further questions or arguing with him. She brought the warm water in a bucket and some cold water in a big mug so that he could brush his teeth as well. She squeezed some toothpaste onto his toothbrush and handed it to him, her eyes glued onto the wounds. She noticed another cut on his neck, the area around the wound swollen and reddish, caked with dry blood.

"What happened? Did you fall from your bicycle at night?"

Impatient with her persistence, he told her half the truth, blinking his one eye to clear his vision. His lips trembled as he bent to clean his face with water. He would never let his wife help him with her rough hands which felt like a fowl's feet. He thought of Lerato, Thandiswa and Shantell, who had a mixture of Zulu and Boer blood in their veins. Those were fine, well-groomed women who always smelt sweet and inviting. His adrenaline pumped hard as he thought of his women who wore brassieres, he bought them. They all did not like cooking and only dined in restaurants.

Senzeni's heart raced but she did not know why. She waited silently. His cleaning opened the deepest reservoirs of his blood from the neck wound which mixed with the soap suds. She fought down the disgust. He gave Senzeni the water mixed with blood to throw away and bring her more clean water. She took the bucket and decided to put some coarse salt in the water to help kill and keep germs away. She took the water and cleaned his body as well, starting with his arms going down. It was then that Senzeni left the hut to prepare some fresh mealie porridge to serve him with his previous day's relish of road runner chicken stew. He did not eat any of the homegrown or wild vegetables. She served him his food which he took with the pretence that he did not see himself eating it.

"Bring me my chilli sauce and salt. How many times shall I teach you how to set the dining table!" he barked with a morsel of food in his mouth.

His idea of a dining table was an old wooden stool balanced on another with the zinc plate of a flattened, small drum which Senzeni often used to dry her vegetables on. He ate in silence with some difficulty. Senzeni looked at him, without saying anything. She thought about her children's birth certificates. Uncle Mthelisi and his mother would surely help her in the matter. Mthelisi was a respectable man even though he worked in the village, rearing goats to sell in Bulawayo. His children went to boarding schools. He had cattle, sheep, donkeys, chickens and turkeys, too. He harvested every season and his children were housed, dressed and warm during the winter nights.

"It is so hot today that fish would come out of the water! Did you sleep well my daughter?" This was MaTshuma pulling a goat skin mat from between the mud wall and a large wooden log fitted to the ground, supporting the cone shaped thatched roof of the house.

"We woke well mother, how about you and the little ones back ho…"

"Ha ha ha, MaKhuphe you have already finished cooking your mixtures of ferments. You must have woken up before the cock crowed! Where is *umhiqo*?"

"Cooling in the open earthen pots in the kitchen. Some is still in the drum. I am so tired I could die from this fatigue."

"That is what lazy women wish. Your daughter-in-law is so lazy she can't even crush the lice on her head. She can't even clean herself up," Uncle Njabulo said lazily, as he cleaned his teeth with an improvised toothpick of thatching grass.

"Njabulo, my son, when will you be cautious and sensitive with your words? Please learn to appreciate and respect other people's children! What have you brought after all those years in South Africa? She has been struggling to keep your home together and you treat her like this! She is also a human being created in the image of Go... hah, my dead father, Njabulo! What happened to you? MaKhuphe?"

Senzeni shrugged. Gogo MaTshuma spit a goblet of snuff as she dusted her torn skirts which were covered by a *sishweshwe* apron before she sat down near Senzeni. She handed Senzeni some dried mushroom wrapped in khaki paper. Senzeni took the parcel with both hands as she knelt to thank her in her totem. She promised to cook them for Bokani who loved mushroom immensely.

"If this had happened when I was in Jozi, they would all be history now. With my unfailing accuracy I could have driven my okapi direct into their bosoms, nx. They could have picked their intestines from the dust. They don't know me!"

Senzeni and MaTshuma tensed their already weak intestines with fear. Fear from imagination. From his apparent ruthlessness, neither of them doubted he could do it. They kept together like a mongrel pack of beings as he continued cursing and swearing. After finishing off his breakfast, he lurched off in the direction of the nearest local bottle store in search of more booze. He disappeared, still muttering swears in his throaty voice.

As soon as he had left, Uncle Mthelisi arrived to check on him. He had parted ways with him the previous night when he brought him home after the brawl at St Joseph's. None of them sympathised with him after hearing the truth of what had happened from Uncle Mthelisi. It was then that the issue of the birth certificates was discussed and they agreed that it was going to be done when Njabulo was gone.

That evening, Njabulo came walking with no borrowed bicycle. He passed through his brother's cattle kraal at the time the herd boys whistled with high pitched notes like referees in a football match, bringing their livestock home.

They did not notice his synchronised step and the swinging rhythm of Njabulo's arms to his feet. Dudu's bicycle had been gambled away as he had done with his. Nobody dared ask Njabulo about it, neither did he volunteer the information. Their suspicions were all correct.

"Mama, when is father going back to Johannesburg?" Hanani asked the same evening.

"I meant to ask too, Mama. When is he going?" echoed Bokani. Senzeni did not reply or show any emotion.

At supper, the children also had chicken instead of just the insides on top of dried cow bean vegetables. Gogo MaTshuma joined them for supper with Uncle Mthelisi and his wife. Nobody joined Njabulo in his special meal of rice and potatoes and pot-roasted curried chicken. Bokani was forced to bring borehole water for him to drink every day after school. Njabulo did not drink water from an open well. "Water with colour. Water should be clear, crystal clear." He would not drink water from that well where Senzeni and the village women let their skirts float. Sometimes they used barrels which they also used to carry their pigs' food in! He would have none of it.

People came from far and wide to help fence Senzeni's field as they had done all the previous years. They worked and ignored Njabulo's crazy tales in his funny accent. He could not even cut a single branch with his late father's axe. He did not have his own. Senzeni was assisted by MaMkandla to pound and prepare finger millet *isitshwala* which they would serve with beans. Everybody ate the meal to their fill and drank beer after finishing the task, chatting away. Njabulo did not have lunch, claiming his stomach was upset, and opted for tea instead.

The weeks Njabulo stayed were like a century to everyone. Senzeni lost another set of goats to the goat hustler to raise Njabulo's fare to Thandiswa, Lerato and Shantell. The money from beer brewing was eroded by his palate which craved refined foods. Even though there was no money for Bokani and Hanna's uniforms, we were all glad when Uncle Njabulo returned to Johannesburg, leaving his wife expecting twins.

Nomvula's Song

I stand on the bedroom balcony of our architectural achievement. It is an Italian style house overlooking the sparkling pool next to the gym house. I hold the bar and the snooker table, thinking of my Paul. Is he still mine? Was he ever mine?

The first time I had seen his car, my saliva flow accelerated for his money. Not for him. I made sure he noticed me and loved me, come what may. The whole day, I stared at him with the hungry eyes of an eagle. To hell with Yvonne. Who did she think she was? Beauty and brains… ha. I am more beautiful than her! And sexy too! Ambuya from Vito Street in Mbare did what she knew best. From the beginning, our marriage had been a three-tier affair like hearthstones. Myself, money and him.

Now, I wallow by the pool all alone like a hippo by the lake. Like a madwoman talking to the invisible. He wanted a wife. I wanted money. I did not care. I had no other way of making it. Me, driving those fancy cars.

Owning a thousand pairs of shoes like Marie Antoinette. I would close my eyes and, with my little finger, touch the next shopping destination from a map in his study. His study, not mine. I would not touch books. Only fashion magazines that I collect on my travels. His secretary would organise tickets and visas within a week. She would also pay all our bills, starting with DSTV. I am tired of the spas in Cape Town. I would try some in Hong Kong and Barcelona.

My mother and all her friends from Mufakose had the task of finding me maids and helpers who never returned to work after their first day off. My maids kept busy, waking up at the crack of dawn and sleeping seconds before midnight.

I have a ring and a certificate for being Paul's other half. I am not sure now if the contract is valid on paper only. In any case, he cannot divorce me. He will lose everything.

After two years of marriage, I made sure I accelerated my speed of producing babies to get attention. Love was getting as tasteless as a spoonful of honey in a mighty ocean.

They say my children are all spoilt. Why not? My husband, their father, has money. What with the mansion we live in. And all the other properties he - oh - we own around the world! Now I stand on the balcony in tears.

Well-manicured lawns and the sparkling pool are a blur in my view. Where is Paul? Who do I ask or tell? The fridges and pantries burst with food. Whoever said appetite is enticed by the presence of food? The wine cellar is packed, the youngest bottle being twenty-five years old.

Should you need to drive, there is a Range Rover, Bentley, Rolls Royce, Ford Mustang, Chrysler, Porsche, and a Ferrari. If you want the fastest ones, Bugatti Veyron and a Lamborghini are waiting in their own garage.

The last time he phoned, two weeks ago, he was in Brooklyn. But that Rebecca, his secretary-cum-PA refused to give me his girlfriend's number. Not that I wanted to phone her!

Hell no, no, no!

What if he divorces me after a scandal? My Paul. Am I married to cars and money? It is true that it was what I wanted. Conjugal rights? A cock or rabbit performs better. It is for duty, once in three months. Seven, even ten months. My husband, Paul.

My sister, I am losing it. I do not want to go to Italy. With whom will I share the wonders of the world that I will see?

Who would pull chairs for me in restaurants in England? I am tired of talking to myself. I want love, not money. Even if I lived in a shack.

I met my ex-boyfriend from high school last week at the shops with his wife and two kids. Their love and laughter were like a mourning song. *Amagugu alomhlaba ayosala emathuneni. Hatina musha panyika.*

Their refusal when I offered to lift them home came as a stab to my heart and soul. Ha! He was driving a Lexus RH 450 Pritchard!

He could have got married to me if I had given him a chance and waited. He did not have money then. Only university assignments and dissertations. I could not wait for that. I double-crossed him with married men. I dated many of them at the same time. I loved money.

He dumped me the moment he caught me being fondled by Mdara Ed in his old Mercedes Benz. I remember him furiously throwing into the nearest dustbin the cheap chocolates and roses he had brought me for Valentine 's Day after bunking his Geology lecture for me.

Pritchard!

His wife is not as beautiful as I am.

I feel dizzy now as I stand on this balcony. Even though the heaters remain on the whole night, I am cold.

Paul, where are you?

That witch of a secretary will not tell me where he is.

She knows all his movements and destinations.

It would have been better if I had made friends with his mother and sisters.

All the women who were in his life before me.

I should have allowed his favourite niece to stay with us.

Surely there is enough food and space.

Now the niece is staying with that Yvonne, the black-eyed witch. Yvonne does not know that I can even sue her!

Do I mean it?

Paul said if I did that, he will give Yvonne the money to pay me and divorce me!

Yvonne! I hate everyone with that name. I curse the maternity nurses who helped her mother deliver her. She helps Paul's niece with her assignments. She did the same degree as her.

Paul's mother stays with Yvonne too. I never said she was a witch. I did not stop my children visiting her at the cottage where she stayed every time she visited. I only did when she had diarrhoea. She was not used to these types of ablution facilities. My mother can stay with me.

She lived in town, yes in Mufakose.

My mother-in-law was not a witch! After raising Paul on beer-brewing money, she became a witch. After sending Paul to university on basket weaving money, she became a witch. It must be that sharp tongued aunt Monde who sold me out. I loved his money yes, but now I love him too. We have children. Everybody can see them.

My sweet Paul. Did you not say that you forgave me when Esther, the maid, forgot to pack the suit and gown you were to wear to your graduation party at Elephant Hills Hotel in Victoria Falls? It was the maid, not me.

I was busy with my manicure whilst she packed. And your child was giving me problems, crying nonstop. You did not want to hear my side of the story. Instead, you poked the open wound by reminding me that I deliberately forgot to pack little Amanda's bridal dress for your sister's wedding. Yes, I had just overslept on my afternoon nap. Everyone makes mistakes!

But you refuse to let me take my nieces and helpers to the village when we visit your mother. If only you knew what flames do to my plastic nails? Besides, I do not know how to build a fire.

I did not say that. I have forgotten how to make a fire. We used to cook on the fire in Mufakose.

Who the hell is this Yvonne? What does she do?

She should find her own husband, not my Paul. Could she be the one who was in the paper the other day? Appointed as Board Chair? What does that mean? A woman? It is all lies. Green blood with a fertile brain! What does that mean? That Sihle, the walking encyclopaedia, the maid I fired. That little upstart! I should have used her to dig information about this Yvonne.

Sihle used to talk in riddles about Yvonne. Mama, Yvonne, the economist flew to Athens. The gardener's wife mentioned something about her working for Yvonne. She kept quiet as I neared their quarters.

Paul can go to her. All my brothers are comfortable with houses in Houghton Park and New Cranborne from the monies they borrowed and never returned to my Paul. I am excited to think about my mother's house that Paul extended.

If I go to the fuel attendant again and risk being caught... The fracas with the gardener from next door still lingers in my mind. Oh! What an affair! It was an overnight wonder!

Where is Paul? Paul, where are you? Come home, Paul. I have developed some love for you. We can still work things out. Leave that agent of erosion called Yvonne.

My Paul.

The whole night you chat with her on Twitter, Skype away with Yvonne whilst I coil myself in an foetal position in the linen bedding I bought in Malaysia, in my sexy lingerie from France, in our bedroom perfumed by Paris Houses of

Fragrance, my featherlight pillows soaking wet with my hot tears. Even when he slept besides me, he would snore like a frog, facing away from me. My Paul. At least now I love you. What do you want from Yvonne which I cannot give you?

What do you talk about with her that you cannot discuss with me?

I am more beautiful than her. Last week I had Indian hair, this week I have Brazilian. Have you seen the pictures I sent you? I heard she has short, natural hair. She does not even use skin lighteners like I do. What does she know about beauty?

My Paul! I never refused to cook the dried vegetables your mother sent you from the village to my kitchen. It is just that the children are allergic to *nyeve, muboora* and *macimbi*.

My husband, Paul. Look at your father and mother. They love each other. Why can't we do the same? Like soulmates. Please, come out of your study for just a minute and talk to me. Come back to me, Paul. You were never hers but mine!

My First Heartbreak

Roman Catholic choir women sounded my father away in song. I could not help but wonder why he had been such a cruel, forbidding man, my father. I doubted he was going to rest in the peace for which the preacher had asked the Almighty on his behalf. My misty-eyed grandmother sat by the graveside of her son. I was surprised at my sudden film of tears. I wondered what my emotions were.

Joy or sadness?

My mother sat down, her head covered in a small blanket, as was customary. As I watched, I was lost in the foggy, frozen memory corners of my mind. My mother, now the official wife. Really? After all those years of being ridiculed and beaten to a pulp by father because she had not been a good enough a wife? If I were her, I wouldn't have worn the damn mourning clothes. I remembered my mother waking up early before the rooster's crow every morning to work in other people's fields whilst he jollied away with MaSikhosana. People had gathered in knots in the moonlight the night of my father's death, whispering rude comments.

Death surely does not sever ties. An old man with a ubiquitous beard looked on pensively at the surrendering of the undeniable imperative of blood as my uncle, who did not talk to my father in his lifetime, worked on laying stones as if to say go and never come back. I am as sure as death itself that most of the mourners were happy the tyrant was gone. I closed my eyes and watched the curtained insides of my eyelids. MaSikhosana moved slowly to sit near my grandmother, much to the sneering of those who could not hide their emotions. Nobody trusted her. It was common knowledge that she ran with the hares and hunted with the hounds.

Suddenly, my mother's swollen face streaked with blood flashed before my face. My soul felt like a fresh boil lanced with a toothpick. Small needles pricked at my mind. I felt my mother was vaguely scandalised by this. I felt like a cold hand had squeezed my lungs out. The old man yawned unconvincingly. I stared stonily on the mound of soil. My mind drifted into the potent spaces of the universe. I found myself away from the scene. A smile crumpled up the tin foil of my delight. I looked down at them with a quizzed smile. I regarded everything with aluminium amazement. I was in a labyrinth. He was dead. A man who never loved his children.

The old man stuffed a fist into his trouser pocket. An average-looking woman whose singing sounded more like farting in an unnatural tune, sat down in the dirt. The mourners stared at her but said nothing. Suddenly, the mourners became as compact and expectant as celebrants waiting to start a riot. How I wished they started it.

MaSikhosana screamed her head off and started talking compulsively, behaving like a murderous lunatic from a satanic institution, speaking of fragrant things. She must have felt like a cat thrown into a deep well. A globule of saliva oozed down her mouth. A fly sucked on the old man's sweat.

I never saw my father smile at us or at our mother. Even when there was something worth celebrating, he was always eager to bring bad news. Even when I received compliments and encouragement from teachers, relatives and other pupils for my distinguished academic abilities, my father never said a good word. My siblings and I could never be worth anything, according to him. Only his children by MaSikhosana would. When we laughed, he accused us of making noise. I never saw my father having a normal conversation with my mother. His words were always accusing and mama would be on the defensive, pleading. Guilt and fear never left me and my siblings. My father sucked out all our confidence from a very tender age.

Mother had borne twelve of us under that devilish yoke and did most of the part of looking after us. My father's actions tore through the faded cloth of my sanity.

Father avoided hard labour, pushing it to my mother and my three brothers who were teens at the time. He treated the boys like his slaves. He left them to attend to wild bulls in the kraal, to tie together strong wild heifers for ploughing. He shouted orders at them whilst he watched from a distance.

I remember one day when father kept shouting at Thabo, my seventeen-year-old brother, to tightly hold the rope which was tied to the heifer's horns. The rope snapped and the heifer charged at Thabo with all its might. Father hid behind a tree, shouting at Thabo to do something. The animal missed Thabo's head by a breath and plunged its horns into the ground. Fiercely, it tossed some dust with its massive horns, raining soil into Thabo's eyes. It then charged into his side, breaking his rib and sending him screaming to the ground. The mad animal made a u-turn and trampled his leg and arm. My mother ran to drag her son out of its way. My uncle, who could see everything from afar, came running with a spear that he jammed into its side. With the pain, the heifer ran away, pushing aside the logs used to close the main gate to gain its freedom. Thabo was left scared out of his wits and bleeding profusely. Mama took off her wrapper and with the help of my uncle, tied Thabo's wounds. Uncle and mama rushed Thabo to hospital in a Scotch cart. My father could be heard cursing, shouting at Thabo for being careless.

To date, my spirit is still in search of the unattainable elixir which my restlessness presaged. The incident also left me with irreverent disgust for him. It was entirely Thabo's fault because he was a stupid boy who spent his time under his mother's skirts.

My father's actions put our sanity under relentless siege and startled me into premature senility. All those thoughts came racing back as I walked with some women from the graveyard to wash our hands in the dish full of herbs placed outside the main gate of our homestead.

MaSikhnosana walked on, rambling incoherently. I felt

that was the price of sending a defenceless woman to a lifetime of writhing agony over the bed of glowing coals she lit for her. Her noise climbed the cliffs of my nerves and crushed my toes. The mourners looked as if they were gagged by the absurdity and completely ignored her. Mother washed her hands and went to sit on the floor of my late father's bedroom. This was sad because she was never allowed to set her foot in that room during his lifetime. It had been MaSikhosana's bedroom. I ignored MaSikhosana who was still sending off a series of hysterical missives and went to sit beside my mother. I joined others for lunch: thick mealie porridge and beef stew. I enjoyed the beef soup as if I was at a wedding feast. My father was dead.

Nobody knew exactly what had happened. He had been swept away by the river and his body was found caught in a tree by the riverbed. Some claimed he committed suicide. Some said he drowned whilst trying to cross. I did not care how he died. The last few years of his life, he had woken up to fight unseen people so much that at one stage he broke all the windowpanes and doors to his room. One could feel that the air around him reeked of guilt. Once the earthquake of those infernal voices came, he would kneel, apologise, wring his hands and plead. The good thing is they visited in the night.

It had rained whilst he was drowning himself in beer at a

tavern across the river. The water had come in a cerebral rage. Skies dribbled compulsively upon the earth, welling up every dry nook and flooding every river. The last person who was seen with him said he left the tavern at around midnight. He claimed father was cursing and threatening to commit suicide. His bicycle was found at the river crossing the following day. He was a man tormented and enslaved by his own actions.

As I sat with my mother, my thoughts drifted, stitching my mind with tongs of lightning, flashes of the dead man's brutalities rushing across. My head felt encased in a fiendish, ice-cold fridge as I imagined what could have been going on in his mind all his life. My thoughts chalked themselves on a black page of a dreamless sleep.

A wispy small cloud drifted contentedly across the sky. A crow hovered. A dish of soiled pots and pans lifted from my mother's head and slid into the deep end of the dark hole. Then the crow pulled father's clothes and tools into the grave. A dove flew in and brought out a clean crisp white cloth and put it on my mother's head. The stitches which were on the cloth, which ran like a great dyke, tore and exposed my mother's face which was glowing like that of a new bride. A strange bright hue flashed in the house the mourners were gathered in. A great charge of lightning exploded in my mind, with a sinister violence, striking the humid air between the clouds and the earth below.

I was woken up by the old man who whispered a gust of

opaque beer as he paid his condolences. My effort to answer him escaped like a cloud of steam out of the crater of my mouth. The man looked like one of those rude and filthy urchins who sang for money at street corners. He had crooked teeth, a foul-smelling mouth and a mean attitude. Barefoot, he walked, exposing cracked feet and dirty coiled nails. He swallowed his saliva with a noise which sounded like a fish splashing clumsily back into the deep river. His eyes protruded from their sockets as if he was startled by an unknown demon. The old vagrant brought his hands together in a clasp as he left the room, leaving the women fanning for fresh air.

My father, the forbidding mountain, broke my heart.

My Golden Breast

The residue of the fine ash particles of my being float and collect on my mother's bosom, landing quietly, one by one, until they form into a human being– me.

I stare into her eyes and they give me assurance that I have landed on the right place, the place where I had developed from the seed planted by my father in her womb, four decades ago. Then, her womb was fertile ground for nine seeds, which sprouted from her a year or two apart. I was the last seed to germinate and come out of her womb. I was sickly, with no hope to live for a day. She tells me she endured some time in hospital for my survival until I was nicknamed after the female doctor who tried all tricks to cure my strange illnesses, including her native German herbs. I experienced stunted growth like maize grown by the invader farmers somewhere in Africa, always lacking the right amount of moisture and nutrients.

She puts her golden breast into my mouth, and I suck deeply and sweat as I fall asleep on her lap. Her golden breast has fed me with assurance, hope and peace. I had told myself I was going to perish in the fight for life. I nearly did. My mother does not ask a lot of questions, no. She feels my pain. Mothers feel their children's pain. When the children are small, mothers hear and feel them cry and silence them with golden breasts. The mothers' breasts twitch and itch, lifting, sometimes even spraying the golden liquid on their blouses when they hear their babies cry.

I do not need to tell her that I am ash. She knows it instinctively, like a calf knowing where its mother's tits are just after falling to the ground from its mother's womb. She tries by all means to make sure I am comfortable. Love radiates from her heart through her golden breast to my mouth, reminding me that I am still a human being, deserving to be loved even though I have nothing to give other than love. I love in my pain and feel loved too. With such thoughts, all my senses and feelings gather in my body, slowly.

I lie like a log in bed as she reads to me. I cannot help her with anything. She understands. She knows I am not lazy. It is just that my limbs are not powerful enough.

Mother knows I have no tears. Ash does not have moisture in it. Her grandchildren went with their mother, who left me sick and penniless. I was not allowed to see them because l had nothing to give to them. My children are fruits collected from a burning tree. Fortunately, fresh fruits do not burn easily. Mother knows that I, her son, am a fighter. She knows that I am twice as brave as Tshaka. I am a son who has stood like a defiant field marshal through the flames which eventually brought him to ash.

She lets him be, as he heals in their compatible silence. Her son has refused to surrender even though he has no strength to fight off the heavy gum-booted feet strutting all over him.

In that state, Father still reports what needs to be done at home and requires money. He is a father. His contribution in bringing me on this earth ended in ecstasy, not mother's nine arduous months beginning with morning sickness, discomfort and ending in indescribable birth pains.

I came as ash but mother wrapped me in her wrapper and suckled me, nurturing me like she did when I came from her womb, many years ago. Father grumbles and complains that I am a useless son. I cannot give him what I used to give him before. He does not even ask where and how my children are. I suppose they are now a burden since I am now a milkless cow. With my father, it is always one way; the one that ends with him receiving. One could get a medal if they ever managed to please him, my unpleasable, unappeasable, ungrateful father. I had disappointed him. Before I had always been as intelligent and reliable as a German Shepherd.

I turn quietly to my ever-waiting golden breast and have a suck. I am a child that nobody loves anymore because I am poor. Life has become a cramping vice. I squirm like a cat in a sack in my mother's blanket every day, often claiming the embrace I so much desire, waking up to the hearty warmth of her kitchen. She tugs her wrapper on her waist and dishes food to me whenever she feels I need the fuel and minerals to bring my nerves back to work. From being ash, my system fights hard and rejects food, instead registering pain, anxiety and fear. This almost tears mother apart, but she will never let me see her tears. Her love for me grows as she shares it freely. "Mother is supreme," like Chinua Achebe wrote.

Today, my mother's love which lasts forever is pacifying my anger at the world. She takes it away, together with the mental energy I possess, with the exhaust pipe of her experience. When I first fell, I was picked by friends and then relatives, because my mother was far away. But they are just relatives and friends, not a mother. My illness could have been judged as pretence for I did not look like a sick person. My strength, which I drew only to fight other flaming issues, could be misunderstood. Other than a mother, the kind of illness could only be understood by some people with big brains, brains as big as their hearts. I did not blame anyone as I withdrew and surrendered to the flames which burnt me, beyond recognition, to the ash. My wife of ten years did not know, when one Monday morning l reported to work to find the gates chained with a sign hanging on the gate. The company was in liquidation. After three months, l came home to find the house empty. Only my clothes, two pots and a gas stove remained.

Positive thoughts flood my mind and heart. I see myself living in the biggest house I have ever seen, with a big office. As they say, there is power in resurrection and I have so much of it. The house is a triple-storey building of Italian architecture, with a mixture of modern and Victorian furniture. It is not only a house but a home. Its picture is so vivid and so alive, one could smell the aroma from its spice-scented Greek kitchen. I plan trips around the world, my first stop the Caribbean Islands, then Bahamas, Nevis then Bermuda. I also think of taking some sabbatical to visit the Plains of Thessaly, the Gardens of Vatican City and Barcelona to learn a bit of Spanish and make new friends. Maybe l will meet someone my mother can call daughter-in-law.

Mother continues to move about with the fluency of nature, tugging and untying her wrapper on her bosom, humming an old village ditty with the inbred courtesy of a tame cat. Her words waft around in the air and return to my ears with re-assurance. It is not the words she is humming which console me but her ancient voice. They seal whatever I had in my mind as true even though I do not utter a word.

After a fortnight of mother feeding me, I regain my body. Every day, I take a stroll in her garden as l regain my strength. I put behind memories of being a symbol of the state of the economy. l had also signed the divorce papers and my wife had already moved in with someone, a man who was a cash baron, and together they were expecting twins.

I could not believe the sudden change of fortunes when a week after that, I opened the hatch door of a waiting plane. Moments later, its gritty shuddering announced its take-off, trembling in its power. It heaved from the ground after running in the direction of Umzingwane River, leaving Bulawayo in a blur.

My eyes become misty as my mouth trembles. I wipe them with the tip of my fingers as I look down at my lap, hiding from the prying eyes of my lady companion who couldn't take her eyes off me right from the departure lounge. Was it a coincidence that we occupied seats next to each other?

In no time, we are high in the sky, shooting between white cotton-like clouds, the nose of the huge bird sniffing at the air above the Limpopo River. Hillocks surrender their sight below as roads appear as laterite tracks. l see homing stock birds which look like flamingos sipping at the dirty water in a pond or a small dam underneath. I am going to sign a multi-million deal with a South African bank. The transaction happened in the twinkle of an eye. I am so dazed with happiness that it feels like a dream.

At the lit airport, I am met by a vivacious lady whom I fall instantly in love with. But not in that sense. I had liked her voice when we arranged the meeting. We manoeuvre away from the faceless travellers as she swings in a sturdy zeal, her short, flared dress top displaying proportional hips under a waspy waistline. She is wearing no tights underneath.

I admire her guts.

Back home, if a woman dresses like that she makes sure she will not walk across a street on her own. It does not matter who you are or what you do, it is a serious crime. Refahliloe Mothaba. I pick her name from the people who stand in line like a posse of horsemen. She helps me with my bag after casual greetings before I bundle myself into her car.

"*Setlatla sa mafelelo* of my husband did not come home again last night," she says cacophonically as she opens the door of her Lexus. She excuses herself from the call and goes behind the steering wheel. I initiate some greeting to her in her mother tongue that I assumed from her name.

"*Ukae*?

"*Ketang, wena*?"

"*Keya ya phela ha e se mokhathala fela*."

"*Hotla loka ho shapa moya o monate* Johhanesburg."

"*Ahe, kiyaleboha kitshepa jalo*."

"You amaze me. You have never lived in South Africa and you speak Sotho so well!"

"I am trying, my sister, to adjust to my temporary environment."

"Typical Zimbabwean. No matter how tough the situation is, you always adjust and survive with humility, patience, hard work and peace. Honestly, I do not think there is a country anywhere in the world with such awesome people."

"Thank you. I like and admire Italians myself especially those from the Vatican City."

Her phone rings.

"Get your stuff and get out of my life, I am tired of y... Hear me clear… listen. I don't have anything to say to you and you leave me alone!"

"Sorry about that. Do you have an unmarried brother? I should get myself a Zimbabwean husband."

"Oh yes, I do. I am flattered."

"l do not know how to respond to this."

"Actually, no. I have a brother who is attending a

conference to do with building Greenhouses in Africa. He is an agro-economist. He is as kind and protective as his words, but he is exactly your opposite. He is quiet and shy."

"Opposites attract, I am ready if he is, ha, ha, ha!" she winks at me. I nearly faint.

"And your husband? Will your ex-husband not come on our tracks?"

"*Khohlwa ngabo labo bhuti*. I have sorted him out."

"Just like that, over the phone?"

"He is a boyfriend. My father has not received anything in his cattle folds from the bastard, yet he has been getting it free from me and many other women for the past three years! *Uyajola*, not a single moment has he been responsible. I used to buy him airtime, imagine!"

"*O na le bana le ena*?"

"Hell no, *bhuti*."

Rain pours in blinding sheets as we enter the vestibules of the bank's offices in Sandton City to staccatos of greetings by the boardroom's anxious occupants. Eggs of hope are already hatching in my mind.

I spend the week that follows house-hunting with Mother. She encourages me that both houses I was going to buy must have a borehole. The house I am to live in should have space so I can grow vegetables, flowers and herbs. She encourages me to employ only two people and a driver. She encourages me to take things slow until I am completely healed.

I keep sucking from my mother's golden breast as I forgive the world.

No Boundaries

I watched the swollen plops splatter violently onto the pavement, mist and little drops of water lifting from the tar and evaporating away.

This was October and those were the first rains. The mist coming off the tar reminded me of people's breath on a cold winter morning and the mighty Mosi-oa-tunya, Victoria Falls. It had been very hot all morning and afternoon. Nobody had suspected rain would come soon as the sky had been very clear. The fluid life of the pavements had come to a standstill. Even the cleaners in red who had been singing gently over the rhythm of their brooms now lined the pavements. Parking attendants mingled with the crowds in their stations.

People watched the rain in awe, their hopes rekindled. I watched everything from the third floor of my office which had no water for ablutions. At least the elevators were not down again and there was electricity. I interlocked my fingers in the manner of prayer and sang softly. The rain had raised my spirits.

Motorists drove carefully, fearing to slide and bump into vehicles ahead of them. The roads were normally slippery after the first rains, with the year's drops of oils which would have fallen from moving vehicles. I would be cautious too. Big muddy bubbles formed in the puddles of water collected in the potholes. It felt cool as the soft rain fell down the window seals, caressing the edges of my memory. I thought of my home and the brown blades of lawn which had dried in the scorching summer heat coming alive again. There was no municipal water to keep the garden and the lawn alive. My hydrangea in the shade of the Msasa tree would talk to me again. I had almost given up on them as I witnessed their pretty lives being extinguished everyday by lack of moisture. Now the swimming pool would fill up and I would use the water to bring them back to life. The garden would thrive again with fresh flowers, vegetables and herbs. Delight flooded my whole being, bringing back my once curtailed hopes. I did not hear the soft knock on the door until the door opened.

"Bekezela, sorry. May we come in?" Mr Dlodlo and his visitor opened the door wider as they came in. My smile had given them approval.

"Oh, I am so sorry I did not hear you knock. I suppose it is because of the noise of the sputtering rain on the window seals. Please, make yourselves comfortable," I said as I moved towards them, my hands stretched for a handshake.

"How are you, Mr Khumalo?"

"I am fine, thank you. And how are you?"

"Doing alright, but business is low. Otherwise, how are things down there?"

"So far, so good. It is hectic all the time."

"It is alright to be busy, you would not like to be like us,

I tell you. I am even thinking of shutting down this one for the time being because it is milking every cent I make elsewhere, until things are alright."

"It shall be alright. I am surprised though at the number of businesspeople coming up here from down South. Every plane landing here is full."

"Is that so? There must be something huge going on behind the scenes then."

"Yes, there is MaHadebe. What do you make of expensive cars on the streets?"

"True, those cars whose passengers never feel the bumpy potholes in them at whatever speed!"

"Drum holes and ravines in the streets."

"Ha ha ha!"

"I hit one along Second Street near the University and lost two tyres and rims last week."

"Where is your freedom then?"

"In the armed injustice."

"1980."

"The war continued in some parts of the country."

"Rwanda."

"Do not be as blind as the locust's eye."

"I was in the village doing grade one."

"You witnessed it?"

"No, I suffered it."

"Then the arbitrary destruction went on, and on, and on."

"Nx," Mr Dlodlo clicked his tongue in disgust.

"Enough of it, Mr Khumalo, shall I organise tea or coffee for you? I know Mr Dlodlo likes coffee. I baked some muffins at home. I hope you will enjoy them," I offered with self-composure and restraint.

"Tea will be fine for me, madam. Thank you very much."

"My pleasure. That will make two of us."

Mr Khumalo's eyes followed all my movements. They were looks that did not pronounce words. I did not feel anything at all about his stares. They had no effect. I took down the telephone hand receiver from my desk to the coffee table in the office.

"Why are you taking the phone down?" asked the visitor.

"It becomes laborious for me to stand up each time it rings. I would rather have it down here."

"Please leave it there."

I did not protest and left it. I just looked at him and wondered. We had tea which Mr Khumalo seemed to enjoy very much. We chatted much about anything and everything. They attended a meeting somewhere in the city.

I was checking my e-mails when they returned. Mr Dlodlo excused himself and left me with the stranger, who, for some moments stared at me motionlessly. I became uncomfortable and began to fidget with my fingers, cracking my knuckles. His stare seemed to see the inner part of my soul. Maybe he was wondering how I could have survived the hunger and disease of this nation; maybe my hair was showing some tinge of orange; maybe he could see the cauterised wounds of my soul and heart. I wondered still at his piercing eyes.

He did not seem to care about my discomfort. He stood up to look at the ruins of my office. There was an exhibition of my life on the wall in pictures. Most were newspaper articles of me either receiving or giving out awards. My humanitarian work. Some pictures were of my interests, and my children, before I had made myself comfortable in this seemingly soothing gloom. Whatever he was looking for, Fezile Khumalo would find it. All the while I followed him, hoping to explain the activities like I had done with other visitors before. I gave up as he seemed not to be interested in any explanation. He turned to look me in my eyes, savouring every moment of it.

"Where is your ring?"

"I am not married."

He gawked again into my eyes. Silence. So silent you could hear a leaf fall. I did not move my gaze from him either. I then decided to answer the unasked questions.

"I have pending applications for my hand in marriage, but I do not know what to do with them. And that picture is of my children, the picture frame over there." I pointed my finger.

"The twins look like you."

"I did not realise. Thank you."

Silence.

Sweat strands ran from his forehead and he took out a clean, cotton handkerchief to wipe his face. I felt sorry and decided to make his life easy.

"High profile businessmen and…"

"I know. High ranking politicians as well."

"How can you say that?"

"Forget them, eh, I mean the politicians." He was placid and indecipherable. He went back to his chair, his eyes fixed on my being.

Mr Dlodlo came in just in time, even though I had a strange feeling he shouldn't have got back just then. I was beginning to enjoy Fezile's serenity. We greeted each other as we picked up our conversation from where we had left it. He suggested lunch and we sent a messenger out to get some. A message tone vibrated on my phone. I opened it and discovered it was from Fezile. It was short and precise. His soul had been lost and found when he met me. His life would be nothing if I could not be with him. Those were his few words.

Butterflies danced in my stomach. I felt as if I was Queen Fabiola of Belgium. I looked at him but did not display any emotion. His eyes met mine. I quickly dashed outside as if to attend to something urgent and important. That had been the reason he had flown in twice before, looking for me, and I had not been available. Once outside, I replied to the message instantly, I told him I wanted true, unconditional love only. If it was not going to be that then I was not available. I sent the message and it reported as delivered before I went back to the office.

The messenger brought in the food and I brought warm water in a jug to wash their hands. I started with the visitor who looked into my eyes and declared, "I am marrying a woman from Zim."

I could have collapsed if I had looked into his eyes; the sudden chemistry was too bold. It was as if I had known him for a decade. After supper, we cleared the improvised dining table. We parted ways soon after that, him and Mr Dlodlo to the hotel and I, home.

I received a message from him after I had taken a bath, whilst doing my bedtime bible reading. The message declared that we were to be partners for life. I was both surprised and happy with the huge commitment. The days and weeks that followed were just for us. We communicated, and we loved each other from a thousand plus kilometres, across boundaries. I forgot my pain. I had no doubt about him despite the boundaries. No problem seemed significant if I thought about him. I forgot about all those applications on my tray. I gave him my heart freely as he gave me his without charge. I glowed as I found new purpose in life.

Before Fezile visited me, I had a vision, so vivid it seemed real. I was sitting on the garden chairs outside one afternoon, enjoying a cool breeze. I had been reading *You Can't Keep A Good Woman Down* by Alice Walker. My mind was free and full of new information.

There I was, standing with my back to the huge, deep dark and ugly gullies and ravines full of hungry crocodiles. I was wearing my elegant outfit that I had bought in Paris. The matching handbag and shoes were from Barcelona, Spain. I looked vibrant and beautiful. An angel stood on my left side and a huge man with white, shining clothes stood on my right. He was showing me a field of ripe sorghum on my left and cotton ready to be picked on my right. A combine harvester was busy at the end of the cotton field, harvesting maize. At the centre of the field was a small hill and suddenly I saw myself with Fezile at its pinnacle, looking at me lovingly. He was in a black suit and I was in an off white wedding gown, my silk veil dancing in the wind as he held my hand. His eyes were full of commitment, love without boundaries. The vision stayed with me for weeks, vivid as it was.

The chemistry happened the time we set our eyes on each other at the airport where I met him the following month when he visited me. We checked into a hotel and sat in the restaurant. He took my hand and once again the flames ignited. He opened his heart to me and told me about his life, his family and his possessions. I was again fascinated by his use of the word "we" in the conversations, talking about our plans for the future. I relished his values which were similar to mine. We coincidentally shared almost the same background.

Nobody took me seriously when I told them about my newfound romance. I threw caution to the wind. I loved Fezile. I waited for him patiently. Only him. Just knowing that he loved me was a good enough feeling for me. We did not need to talk when together, our love for each other was enough conversation.

In spite of all the ugly, discouraging talk, I found myself in the clouds going to visit him for the weekend. We would talk for ages and it was as if we had been with each other an hour before. His looks never changed. We sometimes disagreed and misunderstood each but our love never died. I felt his blood doing things every time I was around him. It seemed his heart disappeared into mysterious caves when I was not around. It obeyed my silent command, as it succumbed to the wait of love, collapsing his limbs.

We were chatting and playing on a flight to Hong Kong when, out of the blue, my stomach started complaining. The pain forced me to spend some moments in the small room.

As I stepped out, I was stunned to see some air hostess and the flight attendants standing along the aisle, holding white and red roses. The strange thing was they were smiling at me. The floor was also carpeted with red roses. I almost turned to a statue when I saw Fezile looking in my direction. His friend Thato who is a pastor and his fiancée, Zanele, were standing on either side of him. Zanele held a bunch of red roses. I blinked away tears as I stood in front of him. He knelt down. Lionel Richie's *I Call It Love* played in the stomach of the huge bird. His piercing eyes injected all his love into my system.

An unknown force had carried me to him. I did not walk

but floated down the aisle, almost forgetting that we were up in the skies, above the vast waters of the ocean. As I reached him, Thato gave him a small golden box.

"*Bekezela, mtaka* Gumede, will you marry me?"

"Yes, I will marry you."

The passengers cheered and threw their roses at me. The world celebrated with us as we landed at Shenzhen Bao'an International Airport from a journey filled with champagne and romance as Mr and Mrs Khumalo.

He later told me that the three seconds he had waited for my answer had felt like a century. Our love knew no boundary.

My Wedding

Muzi Ngcobo was from KwaZulu-Natal, South Africa. He paid *lobolo* a week after proposing and the wedding was set in the two weeks that followed. We had three receptions, first at my village church in Matobo, the second, a traditional ceremony in Kwa-Mashu and the final, in Johannesburg where we were going to live.

I loved him not only for what he was but for what he made me feel when I was with him. He loved me in spite of myself. He grounded me. He had all the befitting qualities to match my character.

I had great joy when I first met Muzi. He said he loved my granite personality. I loved his humility, the calm spirit and the respect he had for mankind, young or old, rich or poor. I loved his integrity and his big heart. He said we had similar personalities. He claimed I had a few amenities that were hard to beat. Muzi hauled me from my shattered self. The truth was I had given up finding true, fulfilling love. It is said that love finds you not the other way round. Love found me. He too echoed the same. Anyway, it is said the most lasting love affairs have inauspicious origins. Ours was instant love. Our love just melted, unstirred.

I met Muzi on a business meeting in Mumbai, India. Whenever we had those meetings, only he and I would be left in the conversation. We talked about the Hong Kong

Stock Exchange down to Equatorial rain forests. We talked about Hiroshima to Caribbean and African literature. We talked about German manufacturers to market gardening in Israel.

Muzi understood that even well-adjusted, self-reliant and pragmatic women like me want to be loved, exclusively. He regarded me as a businessperson extraordinaire. He said he loved the cool professional mannerisms and my spirit. I thought I was just being me. Before I met him, I had kept turning down dates. I felt all the men who asked me out were boys not men despite most of them being highly powered and very rich. I did not want them still. I felt they would not understand me, hence my celibacy.

I had very high standards for a man I would call my husband, a partner for the long haul. I wanted someone dependable, reliable, truthful. I valued integrity and morality. I could deal easily with my man's needs, as long as he was my type. Those who wanted a cheap orgasm, I was simply not interested in. The winning candidate would earn that.

My Muzi did not attempt to tame me. He allowed me to be me. Our grandmothers and mothers were tame enough to let some men run nations to the deep end. He let me be. He never phoned me enquiring after my whereabouts at two o'clock in the morning like they did. He trusted me.

Our wedding was planned in heaven and supported by our ancestors. Even the god of Matobo, the rainmaker, had agreed to it. My favourite uncle held my hand to deliver me to the to man who had paid the bride price two weeks before. Everything was like a dream. I walked as if I was floating in my off-white dress. The decorations were all earth colours, brown and cream. We had no colour theme for our families for the village reception. I just wore my dress for the church and for the village children to marvel. Otherwise, it should have been all traditional dressing. I could not believe I was the one stepping on all layered reed mats to say my vows. To tie myself to this stranger I met about seven months before.

Three bridesmaids followed behind me in cream dresses, looking like angels. Muzi stood near the priest, looking at me as if he was dreaming. I looked into his eyes and could not help a tear welling and misting my eyes. Thousands of pairs of eyes were all set on me, and I could feel my mother and sister weeping from joy. I closed my eyes and watched the curtained insides of my eyelids. I said all my vows after the priest with passion. I looked into Muzi's misty eyes. I could feel his victory as he smiled at me before the priest asked him to kiss the bride. The kiss carried with it some electric current filled. Women ululated, some running up and down, beating the floor with their wrappers. Men whistled and some even blew *vuvuzelas*.

Everybody stood up anxiously as Muzi's uncle requested that the kiss be repeated. Shy as I was, I did not mind it. I loved Muzi dearly.

Muzi was worth the wait. I was drunk with love and the

conviction that I had met love. My Muzi was an exotic species. He was restless as the wind and rootless as a tumbleweed. He moved across the continent and slept in planes and departure lounges but never failed to communicate.

The singing in church took me to heaven's door and back. People danced, threw flowers, rice and sweets at us as we walked away from the church to the car, arm in arm. It all seemed so natural. A fleet of four by fours ferried the bridal team.

I wanted my relationship with Muzi to last far longer than our children were going to be at home. We were to grow white hair together. I was going to adopt an old-fashioned approach to my home life, despite being a busy career woman, maybe leave it altogether. I was going to play second fiddle to my husband. I would befriend his mother, sisters and cousins. I vowed to win their hearts since they were women who knew Muzi better than me. I hoped they would help me win his heart over and over again. I believe love is like fire. From time to time, one needs to put on more firewood and remove the ashes. I wanted mine to keep flowing like a fountain of water in Mtarazi Falls in Honde Valley. I decided I would never bring my old baggage into our home. Our house was going to be a home. Whether in Kwa-Mashu or wherever we chose to live. Nothing would change.

I met Muzi's parents two months before the wedding. His

mother treated me like a daughter from her own womb. The woman was so different from my first mother- in- law who even the angel Gabriel could not please. Even though she had experienced many instances of my thoughtfulness and generosity, she was never satisfied with me. The treatment I got from her was akin to the bounded slaves in the brick fields of Pakistan.

As we landed in Durban, I felt like new wine. I had left my old self in Matobo. I surrendered my identity and acquired a new name, Mrs Ngcobo, which I loved dearly.

The KwaZulu air refreshed us. My gold and diamond ring radiated vividly in the Durban sun. Muzi took me to a romantic stroll by the sea. We chatted and laughed as l reminded him of the way he proposed to me. It had been during our second date when he took my hand suddenly and looked into my eyes. I smiled shyly. He said in a peaceful, calm voice, "Sweetheart, next week I am booking a flight for you to come to Johannesburg. There is a wedding accessory shop I want you to visit. They have everything. After that we are going KwaMashu where my whole family will be waiting for you. You will have to notify my in-laws that I am coming to pay the bride price in two weeks followed by our big day in two weeks."

He pulled his diary from his bag and flipped through the pages, marking dates in circles. I was speechless as tears welled and mystified my eyes. I simply nodded. Muzi poured us some champagne to celebrate. He took both of my hands and asked for a dance. My legs were still weak with shock, so he asked me to sit on his lap instead. We both did not say anything. We sat still, feeling each other's heartbeat.

He took out his phone and dialled.

"*Sawubona*, Mama," he greeted his mother in his native language. "*Ngiyehla nomakoti wakho ngomgqibelo onalo ozayo*. I am coming with your daughter-in-law this weekend."

They talked about other things and you could tell that his mother was excited from the way his face beamed.

The reception at KwaMashu was more electric than the one in Matobo. I was regarded as a very special *makoti*.

Compliments and questions flooded me the whole afternoon as Zulu traditional dances entertained guests. Muzi left me to answer them. He kept on saying to his peers and relatives, "She is now my own. Our own." Echoing their bridal song which went, '*Umakoti ngowethu, siyavuma*.'

I looked at him every time he said that and he just smiled back. The truth is I felt so comfortable and at peace with him, I could not have been with someone else.

The arrangements in the garden for our third reception were just awesome. A small stream with clear water cut across the front yard. One would be forgiven for thinking the stream was natural. The water flowed in it and poured into the swimming pool through the mouth of a marble dolphin. I was amazed at the huge hydraulic stage erected at the reception area facing the tents. The sides were decorated with cream roses. It was a theatre where you could not see the artistes until they emerged from behind the curtains. Red curtains matched the carpet. The ushers were my childhood friends. I wondered when they were trained and groomed for the event. They all carried themselves cheerfully and gracefully. Birds sang melodies as some chirped away at the flowing water in the stream I had secretly named Somoya. I sucked in the tranquillity of the house in amazement.

Suddenly my heart, soul and mind drifted from the scene as I watched the proceedings from a distance, somewhere between heaven and earth. I could see myself with Muzi by my side, playing with my manicured hands, persuading me to come with him to the bedroom which was littered with red roses. Teddy bears sang melodious tunes from Enrique and Sade Adu, *Hero and Lovers Rock*. My soulless body was too shy and over dazed with love to move.

My mind, heart and soul settled back into my frame as I saw the Roman Catholic Church choir belting out my favourite hymn as the stage lifted itself up. They were from my church back home in Matobo.

Then there was lunch and speeches. My childhood friends gave speeches. My aunties and uncles from both our families were also given their chance.

I was more than amazed when I saw a pair of musicians entering the stage through the red curtains. Muzi's brother stood to welcome them and to lead us to the stage. I closed my eyes and Muzi gave me a lasting bear hug. I could not believe it as the duo sang *My Heart Will Go On.*

Tears of joy streamed down my face. Muzi had anticipated what would happen and he wiped them off swiftly.

The lady from the duo took my hand as she sang *I Will Always Love You*. Muzi held my other hand and my heart knocked at heaven's door again. My wedding was planned and arranged in heaven.

My King and Priest

I sit quietly in our garden where birds flap their wings and sing. I watch them drink from the swimming pool, chirping and flying from one spot to another. I enjoy the melodious sounds of water mingling with the songs of the birds. All that makes the place feel natural. I can smell the wet soil. The stream brings the memories of the river in the mornings back in the village when women and girls fetched their first buckets of water.

I watch a pink and yellow butterfly fly over some bright flowers, hesitating to sit on this one or that. Its wings flap very rapidly and colour the environment. Two more butterflies fly abreast of each other, seeking too a place to put their tiny legs, but there is no suitable place for them. If I was younger, I think to myself, I could have chased, caught and collected those butterflies and spent the day talking with them. Up, down and further they go with me back to my childhood. Then the bees come too, hovering around my glass of guava and apricot juice. I hide my face in the wide brimmed hat I had removed and placed on the table. One eventually lands on the inside of the glass and starts sucking on the residue of the drink at the bottom.

I am forty-five and have been married for ten years to my King and Priest, Muzi. Our triple-storey house is situated on a private housing estate in Johannesburg. It boasts a lake on the right and a golf course on the left. It is the finest house in the many suburbs around here. My fingers sweat and leave stains on the glass from which l have been sipping my juice. The bees have sucked the drops of the juice in the bottom of glass . I try to look at the residue at the bottom of the glass but then I drop my eyelids onto a comforting darkness, to measure my frail memory. I wait until my mind is scalded and perfectly free. I moan a lullaby that flows from the sky to the earth, the same blue sky that brushed over my forehead earlier before the bees came. I open my eyelids and see birds still darting casually. The sun steadily ascends into the sky, its rays intensifying the natural feeling which I am accustomed to. Our artificial stream flows on, reminding me of Simpathe River.

I still have homes in Harare and Bulawayo. My businesses are still open and I visit them from time to time, just to check and sign what needs to be signed. The manager comes frequently for meetings with me. I am a serene woman who is a wife and a mother. l love all my God-given duties. I love my King and Priest. I like his concentrated and busy demeanour. His mind and heart seem ever satisfied with me. I am satisfied with him too. I am at complete peace with him.

My emerald and gold-ringed pen drops to the ground. I decide not to pick it up. I look at the dazzling scene of trees, shrubs and flowers that l planted ten years ago, before Khanyelwa and Thozamile were born. They are now casting a sizzling hue from above and beneath. I arrange my books, files and papers before picking up the pen. I quickly take them to the study on the ground floor. I change into my work coat and gumboots and head straight to the garden to join Melusi who is working with his overalls rolled up his sturdy legs, planting young tomato plants. His feet are caked with mud again. I had since stopped asking him why he never liked working with his gumboots on. The skin on his arms pulsates up and down, showing bands of muscle. Melusi is a quiet and gentle boy, also from North of South Africa, just across the Limpopo. At nineteen, he is a breadwinner to his siblings who are being looked after by their aged grandmother. Twice, Melusi has told me that I remind him of his late mother, and the remark does nothing but well my eyes. He dropped out from Mzingwane High School where his parents also worked.

Near the herb garden, I get stung by a nettle. I often make tea for Muzi with its leaves. The itch lasts a few moments, reminding me of the *imbabazane* shrub. The good thing about this stinging nettle is that it is a good preventer of prostate cancer. I watch the petunias and mauve protean talk to each other by the corner of the pool. Along the stream, red, white and cream roses dance to the wind which is blowing calmly. All the flowers in the garden are vibrant. We had wedged in between them tiny pebbles of different colours and across the stream we had planted some lawn and a poster which reads:

Inside the letters we placed some small stones l had picked from the beach in Cape Town. They are blue in colour and they blend well with the green lawn and white lilies l brought from the Eastern Highlands of Zimbabwe where they grow in the bush.

In the pool, water flows out of the mouths of two big marble fish, pouring into the pond. They are a gag novelty. The water mixes before it flows away around the garden through the artificial stream we created. I had planted some riverine vegetation along the stream, but only the combretum bushes and faidherbia survived. The ficus died and what remained grew stunted. In the pond, we put small tropical fish: cod, tiger, silver and redfish. I watch them as they swim up and down, hiding under the sea weeds, breathing through their gills.

We had planted some redolent eucalyptus trees along the driveway. They discharge some pleasant aroma which blends with that of lemon trees in the orchard. Their scent combined is heavenly. Muzi loves sitting in the garden too. I think of him as their scent tickles my nostrils. Purple jacarandas also line the boundary of the yard from inside. We do not sweep the purple flowers away, we just manage them.

My lips itch, betraying the need for some lip gloss. I fetch some from my work coat pocket and apply slowly, enjoying their lemon scent and feel. I then flick some pebbles into the pond to enjoy their plop sound and to see the fish scurrying away. Their movement liberates me, giving me some peace. I sometimes wonder what he saw in me! I was never like him. Even though we shared the same values, he was calm and I, the opposite, very cheerful and energetic. I had changed through being with Muzi. I am serene and content with his love.

I take a set of pliers from Melusi and snap at the flowers, tying those which need tying and pruning the wayward ones. I cut some at their grooves. I enjoy looking at the evenly laid flower beds. I remove some roots with spindly tentacles protruding outside the beds, making them uneven. I move from flower bed to flower bed, Melusi following me, doing what I instruct him to do. I truly enjoy these moments. Birds continue singing. A ladybird moves up a plant and I let it be. In this part of the City of Gold, one can only hear a gate opening. The air is fully refreshing and the place is full of the aroma of fresh flowers.

Muzi, my true King and Priest, plucked me off the hills, rocks and boulders of Matojeni, from the trees and rivers of Matobo which knew me by my scent and laughter. I am a stabilising anchor that put his life on an even keel. He does the same to my life. Our love was intense right from the beginning. It was the third companion in the house, before the kids were born. Our life together is not a game of intricate deceptions and misunderstanding. We are a welcome interlude to each other. I am his Queen, a true African Queen and mother. I never search through his phone, his diary or his emails. I am comfortable that the kids are fed, sent to school and housed. Above all, he invites me to all his important trips, business or social. I am his advisor, lover, everything. I love his sobriety. Muzi gives me my position.

We visited Khulu and gogo Ngcobo up in KwaMashu during the holidays and stayed to help in the fields and spend time with them. He would call from Europe or the Middle East and speak with them. His mother is still my friend. So are his sisters and aunties. There is no war of attrition between me and his sisters.

Muzi, my King and Priest. I am not the kind of woman who clings, controls and will not let go of her man until his pockets are torn. I do not burst his eardrums with nagging. Our bedroom is not like a love nest girdled with thorns and red-hot charcoal. I enjoy working from home. I cook for him, do his laundry, serve him food. I have a helper and cook but l still do everything for my husband. He likes his food and enjoys my recipes as much as he enjoys what his mother and sisters taught me to cook for him. I must have made my way into his heart through his stomach too, as advised by the ageless autochthon of knowledge. Muzi is a clean man. There is not much effort from my part as I am also allergic to dirt. I am on close terms with my washing machine and the ironing board. Even my hairdresser can count on my loyalty.

Muzi is a dapper dresser, every inch a gentleman. Like an animal avoiding the lair of a predator, he approaches the study I work from with measured caution. He enjoys my work. He does not even carry himself with the unconscious pomp normally associated with men of secure means. Despite not being at home most of the time, my King and Priest Muzi has an intense paternal sense. The kind I dreamt of since I discovered I was a woman to be married one day. He is not a man of austere tradition and regiment. He spends money on his family, spoiling his queen and children alike.

Muzi does not want me to have trouble meeting him at the Airport whenever he comes from his business trips. At first, I thought he was hiding mischief. Then I thought even if he had somebody that he travelled with, how would I possibly see and know them in the crowds. We never scream at each other. We never call each other names. He knows I am not a womb without a brain.

Once in the house, after picking the kids up from school, l sit in the study to prepare a paper I am going to present at the Makerere University in the next week. I look at our wedding picture taken on our day. I was walking down the aisle of the church back home. Muzi was waiting anxiously for my father to hand me over to him. It is our tenth anniversary today. I have written a poem for Muzi and invited his friends to write him letters which they will read to him. I will send for an *imbongi* to read and perform for him during the dinner that I am preparing for us tonight.

As Muzi comes out of the garage, the *imbongi* starts reciting a poem, moving around, in front and besides Muzi:

Because of you I have forgotten my name
And re-christened myself
I have walked back on my convictions
Because of you
I left behind my ancestors' graves
Adopted your mother tongue as my own
Your rivers, ravines and trees
Know my laughter and hear my voice
They smell my scent
And recognise my footprints
Because of you
The mention of your Province makes my blood rush
Pumping my adrenaline with the highest voltage
bringing breezes of fresh air
making me dance under the African sun
Caressing the ground
Where your cattle and goats walk on
With my feet
Because of you
I only want to drink water from your rivers
And from wells your ancestors dug
I want to eat the wild berries you ate
Savouring their taste with the memory of our encounter
Our first kiss

Because of you
My life has meaning
Your love has reduced my age by half
My beliefs and ways now suit yours
Blended together like honey
Honey the definition of our love and life
Those who had opposed our love
Had rocks and walls to warn
Hold my wasp-like waist
Caress my bottle-like legs
Enjoy my African curves
Bring my mouth to yours for a kiss
And turn me to a riot tonight
Hold on to my gracious step
My infectious laughter
Embrace my love and warmth
And let me mother your clan
And give them fresh produce from my womb
For that is my love's giving
Take my hand and fly with me
Across the oceans where you go
I love you, sweet Muzi
Do not touch the dial
Let the music flow
I love you today, yesterday
And forever
On you, my heart and its dregs

I have poured
In the wilderness of nature
Lies my sweet love
Forever ready for you

By the end of the poem, Muzi is in tears. He cannot hold them back or look at me. His sister and friend lead him away into the bedroom. She cannot believe what she sees there, either. The bed and floor are a carpet of red roses and petunias from our garden. White and cream roses are arranged in a statement which reads:

Muzi and Bekezela
A decade of love
Partners for life

The camera guy follows it all in awe, filming away. Muzi sits on the settee in the bedroom with his hand on his head. He asks his friend to call me. He demands privacy so only the two of us remain. I look into his eyes.

He is guilty as charged. My heart breaks but I manage to bring myself together as usual. I feel it is not the right time for such talk, but I listen all the same and make sure the sound and the contents of his speech may not depart without substance.

"Did you use protection?" I ask him calmly.

He cannot open his mouth. I look at him, seeking a

response. He cannot look at me. He just nods. I kiss him on the cheek and hug him. I can feel his heartbeat. I know him so precisely. I am so close to him that I could hear all his dreams at night and tell him about them in the morning. I lead Muzi out of the bedroom to the lounge where his favourite song is playing.

We join the other people around the dining table. Muzi sits so close to me it looks like we are glued together. I feel the chemistry I felt on our first date. I serve him his favourite meal from the buffet dinner I have prepared. He softens up and slowly picks conversation. He is surprised to see his son from the previous marriage. He is surprised too, to see his childhood friend he herded goats with, back in KwaMashu where he played in the sands on the riverbed.

His father stands up, leaving his food to fall onto the floor, and pulls his long-time sweetheart to the dance floor. Everybody cheers the golden couple.

Muzi searches my eyes. I nod in assurance that I have forgiven him as we stand on the dance floor. My husband, my love, my King and Priest.

GLOSSARY

Ke'ng mme (Sotho): What's the matter mother?

Ngoane (Sotho): It is a child

Laat ons line (Afrikaans *Tsotsital*): Let's go

Orra nna (Sotho): You mean me

My maar hoor my (Afrikaans): I swear by my mother

Morena oa ka (Sotho): My Lord

Eya mme (Sotho): Sure mother

Asseblief (Afrikaans): Please

Likayi mme (Sotho): How are you mother?

Ke'tang sisi wena (Sotho): I am fine my sister how are you?

Uyateta khona eZim ne (Zulu): Are you going to deliver your baby in Zim

Uyatsiba (Sotho): He knows

Setlatla sa mosadi (Sotho): Fool of a woman

Sekuru (Shona): Uncle

Malayitsha (Ndebele): Courier, Porter

Askies sisi (Afrikaans, Tsotsital): I am sorry

Imihlolo yami bantu (Ndebele): An exclamation used when something mysterious happens

Kiyareboha (Sotho): Thank you

Utsamaye sinhle (Sotho): Go well

Kragdadigheid (Afrikaans): opposed to diplomacy, brute force

Mkwasha (Shona): son-in-law

Maiguru (Shona): aunt, sister-in-law

Mdara (Shona slang): Old man

Mari handina (Shona): I have no money

Mzukuru (Shona): niece or nephew

Lingabongimbuluzela mina (Ndebele): Do not make a fool out of me

Ntambama (Ndebele): evening

Umcaba (Ndebele): fermented milk mixed wth boiled ground sorghum

Incukuthu (Ndebele): sharpened iron rod Ukhezo (Ndebele):

wooden spoon

Ekhutheni (Ndebele): an enclave made logs usually build in the front of a homestead

Kuyini (Ndebele): what's the matter

Nholowemizana (Khalanga): a custom which was practiced by The Khalanga's where a new bride was supposed to sleep with her father - in – law before sleeping with her husband

Kolema (Khalanga): It is tough

Sokwedlule (Ndebele): it is over

Mkhwenyana (Ndebele): son - in –law

Asimfuni thini (Ndebele): we do not want him

Mfowethu (Ndebele): my brother

Akazvarwirwa (Shona): a custom where indebted parents would offer their daughter as a way of clearing the debt

Isitshwala (Ndebele): thick porridge made from maize meal, sorghum floor or finger-millet

Inkobe (Ndebele): a meal made from boiling roundnuts, cow beans and maize

Ke ya phela ha e se mokhathala fela (Sotho): I am fine it's just that I am tired

Hotla loka ho shapa moya omonate Johannesburg (Sotho): you will be fine after breathing Johannesburg fresh air

Sawubona mama (Zulu): hello mother

ACKNOWLEDGEMENTS

Special thanks to my friends to whom l read the first draft of this collection of stories: Musaemura Zimunya, Jerry Zondo, Shimmer Chinodya, Memory Chirere, Monica Zodwa Mupambawashe-Cheru, David Mungoshi and Sekai Nzenza. I especially acknowledge Prof Maurice Vambe, Prof Prudence Khumalo, Dr Everisto Benyera, and Prof David Mutasa for their encouragement. I also thank my niece, Zibusiso Ngwenya, and Sicelo Ndlovu for typing the first stories. My unending love to Lazarus and Hungatani Bvirakare. Thank you, Tatenda Tinso Bvilaz for everything, and all those who gave me support, ideas and strength to continue writing. I also thank those who doubted I could do this. May the Almighty God bless you abundantly.

CREDITS

Chinua Achebe, *Arrow of God* and *Things Fall Apart*; Alice Walker, *You Can't Put a Good Woman Down;* Harry Belafonte Oliver Mtukudzi; Thomas Mapfumo; Black Mambazo; R. Kelly Rihanna; Beyonce; Zahara; Mafikizolo; Enrique; Sade Adu; Celine Dion.

ABOUT THE AUTHOR

Tsitsi Nomsa Ngwenya is the author of *Izinyawo Zayizolo* (2016), the award-winning *Zal'Abantu Ziy'Ebantwini* (2022), and *Portrait of Emlanjeni (2023).*

The Fifty Rand Note is her 2nd publication - a collection of short stories that was first published in 2017, and this is the 2nd edition, which has cemented her place as an exciting voice among the current generation of Zimbabwean writers. Two of the stories from *The Fifty Rand Note* were initially published in *Imbizo*, a UNISA journal, in 2014

There is no doubt that Tsitsi's profession as a town planner has allowed her to create stories with care, designing worlds with the ease and effortlessness of a tour guide. The result of such careful planning are stories that allow readers to not only read, but also experience the worlds she designs.